SPIRI

C000303436

THORSONS
PRINCIPLES
OF

SPIRITUALISM

LYN GUEST DE SWARTE

Thorsons

The publishers would like to thank
Jillie Collings for her suggestion for
the title of this series, *Principles of...*

Thorsons
An Imprint of HarperCollins*Publishers*
77–85 Fulham Palace Road
Hammersmith, London W6 8JB

The Thorsons website address is: www.thorsons.com

Published by Thorsons 1999
3 5 7 9 10 8 6 4 2

A catalogue record for this book
is available from the British Library

ISBN 0 7225 3813 8

Printed and bound in Great Britain by
Caledonian Book Manufacturing Ltd, Glasgow

CONTENTS

INTRODUCTION

Spiritualism is a religion, a science, a philosophy and a way of life; not only is life eternal, but this can be proved.

As a religion it is progressive and is considered by many to be the mother of all religions.

As a philosophy it is clear and accessible, and as a way of life it brings an element of joy into every nook and cranny of everyone's pathway through life on earth.

Spiritualism itself was born of the northern hemisphere of our planet, although its phenomena are universal and timeless and the truths that it has revealed are as old as the earth itself.

So how does Spiritualism prove that every human being, as well as every other, creature lives for ever?

This is established through mediumship.

It is established through those dedicated people who develop their psychic abilities to such an extent that they are able to make a link, to become the exchange whereby those who presently reside in the world of spirit may communicate with those still here in the world of physical matter.

Our psychic being is our intuitive self. It is that aspect of our persona that knows what we like and what we dislike – and not only that, very often whom we like and whom we dislike at a first meeting.

All of us can recall walking into a building, whether it be someone's home or a public place, and feeling immediately uncomfortable, or walking into a crowded room, perhaps at a party, and seeing somebody that we like the look of or feel drawn to for no particular reason. Or the experience of making up a foursome for your friend's benefit, a so-called 'blind date' situation, where you are then forced to be in the company of someone to whom you have taken an immediate dislike for an entire evening. All these impulses emanate from your psychic faculties.

This psychic side of your earthly life has a direct association with your spirit, and through your spirit to the spirit dimensions.

WHAT IS THE RELIGION OF SPIRITUALISM?

Like every other religion, Spiritualism is founded on psychically received information about the meaning of life. Like other religions, it is founded on how to achieve at least a modicum of spiritual success in this life, leading to an even more successful afterlife.

The main difference between Spiritualism and other similarly revelatory religions is that in Spiritualism the revelation demonstrates that all sentient beings continue consciously to exist after the physical transition we call death, unconditionally.

Spiritualism has no Messiah, either gone before, here now, or expected in the future. Neither does Spiritualism require anyone to participate in any ritual or ceremonial in order to enjoy its benefits.

Ever since time began Spiritualism itself could be said to have struggled to get through to the consciousness of the world at large. The ancient civilizations had all heard of the existence of the world of spirit through psychically gifted individuals living among them at the time. The belief systems of the Incas in South America, the Greeks, Romans, Babylonians and Egyptians, and after them the Israelites, who perhaps produced the most famous psychically and spiritually aware communicants with the world of spirit, all owed their beginnings to such spirit-transmitted information. However, right up until the middle of the 19th century the message of unconditional life after death, and that we are all spirit here and now, and then and there, was suppressed by those who held the reins of power. What is more, the ruling establishments made it their business, in the interest of their own materialism, to misappropriate and misrepresent what was being given to them. And so the world rolled on, with all the different religions being easily manipulated into becoming warring factions. Little by little the human race was also becoming a little less accepting of the mostly dreadful conditions they were expected to live under, courtesy of the top dogs. Thus the scene was set for revolution...

THE HISTORY OF SPIRITUALISM

In 1848, while in Europe the majority's discontentment with their lot was boiling over into bitter and bloody revolution, and the anti-slavery abolitionist lobby were intensifying their campaign in the United States, something unusual was happening in a cottage in Hydesville, New York State.

The Fox family had been living there some little while, and were becoming increasingly disturbed by noises and bangings in the house that didn't have any apparent source.

On the night of 31st March, the bangings, the noises that sounded like pistol shots, were so loud that two of the daughters of the family couldn't sleep at all.

One of them had the bright idea of assuming that there really was somebody making the noises, and they decided to call this somebody 'Mr Splitfoot'.

'Come on, Mr Splitfoot, do as we do,' said Margaretta and Kate, clapping their hands.

The bangs echoed the noise made by their clapping.

As soon as the girls realized that even though they couldn't see the person who was communicating in this way with them, that he could obviously hear them, they used the now famous command, 'Knock twice for yes and once for no.'

The two teenagers then devised another simple code for the

alphabet. By this means they were able to hold a 'conversation' with a man who told them that his name was Charles B Rosna, and that he had been a travelling salesman staying with some people called Bell, in that same cottage, some years before the Fox family had moved in.

He told the Fox sisters that he had been murdered, that his stock and personal belongings had been stolen and that his body was buried in the cellar. He also mentioned a tin box that was with his body. During this amazing episode Mrs Fox had come into the girls' bedroom. The girls explained what they were trying to do, and Mrs Fox undertook her own little experiment. In order to find out whether Mr Rosna could see them as well as hear them, she clapped her hands silently, and asked him to repeat in knocks of his own the number of times she had put her hands together. The answering knocks came back correctly.

The news of this psychic happening spread like wild fire. People came from all around to experience at first hand this contact with someone, an ordinary person, who was without a doubt dead, but somehow still in communication with the living.

The most remarkable aspect of all this psychic activity was the sheer unremarkableness of the original recipients of Charles Rosna's communication. The three Fox sisters (Leah hadn't been at home that first fateful night, but later participated in the 'inter-world link-up') were young teenagers, unworldly, and with only basic education. Nor were they particularly religious or saintly.

This prompted others to make attempts to contact the world of spirit for themselves, and soon many groups were sitting together in homes all over America, hoping to hear from their dear departed. Many met with a good measure of success. Meanwhile, when the cellar at the Fox home was dug up, a peddler's remains were discovered – and a tin box.

As people gathered together in these convened circles, so it became clear that various members were perhaps more able to facilitate the required link with spirit than others, and so mediumship began to burgeon among the general population – albeit that part of it that was positively psychically inclined. The Fox sisters developed their mediumship further, and found themselves much in demand to talk about their psychic experiences, spiritual revelation and, of course, to demonstrate publicly their ability to communicate with people on the 'other side' of life.

EARLY OPPOSITION

Now, none of this was taking place without opposition – but although the religious fundamentalists tried to invoke biblical prohibitions against Spiritualist practices – and practitioners – somehow the spirit of freedom prevailed against these repressive forces.

Then there were the atheistic debunkers. Although the names of the most vehement and articulate of these are well known to us now in the 20th century, in the 19th their atheism was not something they dared shout about.

Nevertheless, part and parcel of the American dream – and its Bill of Rights – does allow for freedom of worship, and churches were set up to provide regular and safe venues for the exponents of mediumship, for the newly delivered teachings from those in the spirit realms of a higher order, for the further development of earthly mediumship and as a social meeting place for those of like mind.

By 1852 many Spiritualist societies were operational, and had attracted the interest of many scientists and scholars. There had been material verification of Charles Rosna's account to Margaretta and Kate Fox, and in that year an American medium,

only ever referred to, in the fashion of that time, as 'Mrs Hayden', brought Spiritualism to Britain.

SPIRITUALISM IN BRITAIN

As you might have expected from the gentlemen (as they all were then) of the third and fourth estates – pulpit and press – in the land that saw off the Pilgrim Fathers and their families in the *Mayflower* they lost no time in their persecution and abuse of this returnee, a member of yet another non-establishmentarian religion.

Mrs Hayden was, however, equally strongly defended by such distinguished public figures as the socialist Robert Owen, the founder of the Co-operative Movement who had become a Spiritualist himself after an evidential sitting (a sitting with a medium which provides evidence of survival in the spirit realm – such as recollections known only to the enquirer and the person who has passed into spirit) with this pioneering medium.

Only one year after Mrs Hayden had arrived on British soil the first Spiritualist church was established in England, at Keighley in Yorkshire. This church is still called the 'Mother' of all Spiritualist churches in Great Britain.

Over the next 20 years, many Spiritualist churches and societies took root, during which time the first Spiritualist newspaper, *The Yorkshire Spiritual Telegraph*, was published, the prestigious Dialectical Society published a favourable report on its investigation into Spiritualism, and scientist Sir William Crookes reported on Spiritualism to the Royal Society. Meanwhile, the British National Association of Spiritualists – now known as the College of Psychic Science – was founded in London in 1873. Perhaps most significant of all for present day Spiritualism, a scholarly, professional and widely travelled woman, Emma Hardinge Britten, had developed her faculty for mediumship and had become a Spiritualist. Ms Hardinge Britten used her considerable intellectual abilities in the service of Spiritualism, writing several books on the subject, exercising her expertise as an orator and touring in America, Australia and Britain, lecturing and of course demonstrating the spirit communication that her chosen religion was built upon.

In 1871, Emma Hardinge Britten received the 'Principles of Spiritualism', from her erstwhile defender, friend and colleague, who had by that date passed on to live in the spirit world, Robert Owen.

THE PRINCIPLES OF SPIRITUALISM

These Principles, seven in all, were later adopted by the Spiritualists' National Union (SNU), the recognized religious organization representing the religion of Spiritualism in Great Britain.

These particular Seven Principles are:

1 The Fatherhood of God
2 The Brotherhood of Man
3 The Communion of Spirits and the Ministry of Angels
4 The continuous existence of the human soul
5 Personal responsibility
6 Compensation and retribution hereafter for all the good and evil deeds done on earth
7 Eternal progress open to every human soul.

Back in the birthplace of modern Spiritualism, the American National Spiritualist Association of Churches (NSAC) also has a similar set of Principles, nine in number. They are:

1 We believe in Infinite Intelligence.

2 We believe that the phenomena of Nature, both physical and spiritual, are the expression of Infinite Intelligence.

3 We affirm that a correct understanding of such expression and living in accordance therewith, constitute true religion.

4 We affirm that the existence and personal identity of the individual continue after the change called death.

5 We affirm that communication with the so-called dead is a fact, scientifically proven by the phenomena of Spiritualism.

6 We believe that the highest morality is contained in the Golden Rule: 'Whatsoever ye would that others should do unto you do ye also unto them.'

7 We affirm the moral responsibility of individuals and that we make our own happiness or unhappiness as we obey or disobey Nature's physical and spiritual laws.

8 We affirm that the doorway to reformation is never closed against any human soul here or hereafter.

9 We affirm that the precepts of Prophecy and Healing contained in all sacred texts are Divine attributes proven through Mediumship.

OTHER SPIRITUALIST SOCIETIES

Even though the NSAC in the US is a huge network of affiliated churches, centres and organizations, there are still countless hundreds of other societies which have their own particular concept of how Spiritualism should be interpreted and practised.

Likewise in Great Britain there are many independent organizations, such as the Greater World Christian Spiritualist Association (GWCSA), formerly the League, started by Ms Winifred Moyes on 30th May 1931, at the behest of her special Guide from the spirit world, known as Zodiac, who gave his first public address through her trance mediumship in August 1928.

The GWCSA enjoys the affiliation of many churches whose members make this Declaration of Belief and Pledge:

1 I believe in one God who is Love;
2 I accept the Leadership of Jesus Christ;
3 I believe that God manifests through the Illimitable Power of the Holy Spirit;
4 I believe in the survival of the Human Soul and its individuality after physical death;
5 I believe in the Communion with God, with His Angelic Ministers and the souls functioning in conditions other than the earth life;
6 I believe that all forms of life created by God intermingle, and are interdependent and evolve until perfection is attained;
7 I believe in the perfect justice of Divine Laws governing all life;
8 I believe that sins committed can only be rectified by the sinner himself, or herself, through the redemptive power of Jesus Christ, by repentance and service to others;
9 I will, at all times, endeavour to be guided in my thoughts, words and deeds by the teachings and example of Jesus Christ.

The Spiritualist Association of Great Britain (SAGB) is another large organization promoting mediumship in all its forms, just like all the others. The SAGB has close ties with some of Britain's most august persons: Air Chief Marshall Lord Dowding and Lady Dowding; Sir Arthur Conan Doyle; Lady Doyle – who continued Sir Arthur's mission to spread the word of spirit communication and Spiritualism after he passed to spirit himself – and Sir Oliver Lodge, to name but a few.

Another significant Spiritualist conclave, with Principles encompassing a belief in reincarnation, is the one instituted by

another pioneering medium, Grace Cooke, with her Guide White Eagle supplying the initial inspiration and instruction. Called the White Eagle Lodge, it is Grace Cooke's descendants and their partners who are now at the helm of this organization.

Among all these giants, it's perhaps easy to lose sight of all the smaller associations and groupings, such as the Corinthians and the United Spiritualists among others, as well as the independently-run single churches who often have a substantial membership and following, that are also part of Britain's Spiritualist heritage. They are the real non-conformists in the Spiritualists' midst.

THE LEWISHAM (INDEPENDENT) SPIRITUALIST CHURCH

One such is a smallish white building behind a public house in Boone Street, Lewisham, southeast London.

It has remained staunch in its resolve to mind its own business – Spiritualism – since it was founded in 1936 by Henry Hall, William Brewer and John Riches.

This church is a hive of Spiritualist activity six days a week. Apart from one Divine Service on a Sunday at 6.30 p.m., the other days are taken up with healing and readings both for groups and individual private sittings, all on offer from trained healers and mediums out of the many specialist-led and -taught development circles held there.

The resident healers and mediums have all spent a minimum of two years sitting in circle (a 'circle' is the common name given to the small groupings of people who sit together in order to develop their own psychic gifts and spiritual aspirations, usually with a view to making their own contact with those in the spirit world) every week without a break, and are considered to be still training if it is decided that they are of sufficient standard to offer their services to the public for a further two-year period, week on week without a break.

All the work undertaken in the church is for the benefit of the church and those who use it, whether regulars, newcomers or casual visitors.

There are regular special evenings of mediumship, advertised locally, as well as bazaars and other fund-raising and charity events.

The policy is to welcome all to Spiritualism, no matter from what culture or faith. They ask no one to put aside their own religion in order to come into the church, or to worship on a Sunday.

At Lewisham it is avowed that Spiritualism is a way of life, and that declaration is displayed in the way the church conducts itself for all to see.

There are churches like this dotted around the country. Part of the enjoyment of being a Spiritualist, or wanting to find out about Spiritualism in a practical way, is to search out and visit several different Spiritualist churches and centres – including those that aren't affiliated to the larger Spiritualist societies.

This searching is also a less mind-taxing way to exploring some of the tenets of the Spiritualist philosophy...

THE PHILOSOPHY OF SPIRITUALISM

I t's often been said that the philosophy of Spiritualism is contained within the wording of the Seven Principles (*see page 5*). These Principles, by the way, used to be qualified by the legend 'With Liberty of Interpretation'. This appended motto was abandoned in 1988, as it was pointed out to the Spiritualists' National Union (SNU) by its legal advisors that in law they could not have additions or amendments to the statement of belief contained within their Memorandum of Association. In any case, this 'Liberty' had given carte blanche to some very strange interpretations.

There are more and more objections being raised about the wording of these Principles within the philosophy of Spiritualism itself. Many Spiritualists take exception to the archaic concept of a God personalized as a father figure. Suggestions have been made for the term 'parent' or 'awareness of God' rather than 'Fatherhood of God'.

Others argue that 'The Brotherhood of Man' is surely now outmoded as a blanket phrase, which could be better declared as the 'Kinship of the human race and all God's creatures'.

In addition, queries have been raised regarding Principle 4 – 'the continuous existence of the human soul'. Why, it is being asked, would only the human soul enjoy a continuous existence?

In spite of these minor disagreements and dissensions, Spiritualists believe that the mainstay of their way of life is the philosophy of unconditional love.

As befits a free-thinking religious movement, there seem to be as many subtle – and some not so subtle – philosophical differences as there are people. Although of course birds of a feather will flock together, so it does make it easier to discover which philosophy is followed or accepted, and by whom, when such groupings exist.

There are many philosophical teachings and treatises now in existence, given through mediumship – some through one regularly-used medium by one specifically identified communicator from the world of spirit, and some given to be written down or spoken at the time by a random mediumistic availability (that is, someone who possesses the mediumistic faculty and is available at a particular time for a communication from one in a higher plane of existence, almost as a 'one off', for the communicator – and the receiving medium).

As earthly Spiritualist philosophers go, the one who in his time stood head and shoulders above the crowd was Arthur J. Findlay.

ARTHUR J. FINDLAY

Findlay was not a medium himself, he was a classics scholar who took advantage of his own wealth to retire from the family brokerage business in order to make a study of every aspect of Spiritualism including mediumship and comparative religion.

Findlay was born in 1883 and passed to spirit 24th July, 1964, aged 81. He wrote many books, his most famous being his 'Trilogy', and within that the most heralded of all, *The Rock of Truth*.

He was a progressive man, although the assumptions made in some parts of this book about the intellectual abilities, intelligence and culture of the working classes, and black people in the US, reflect the general social unawareness of a gentleman in his position in the 1930s.

He therefore wrote in the terminology, and using references, more suited to his time than the present, and yet his concepts are sound and his scholarship almost unassailable.

In this passage from *The Rock of Truth*, Arthur Findlay discusses the Fifth Principle of Spiritualism, Personal Responsibility.

It is easy to be wicked if you are not to be held responsible for your misdeeds. It is not difficult to defraud your neighbour, if you feel that all you have to do is to ask forgiveness and believe that Jesus took your sins away and suffered for them two thousand years ago. The possibility of transferring your sins to some other person, or creature, is a very old delusion. Most of us know the Old Testament story of the paschal lamb, which was killed as a sin offering. The Arabs had similar custom, and the belief in a sacrificed saviour is to be found in many of the world's religions.

This belief was general throughout the east at the time of the early Christians, and gradually the idea developed that Jesus took the place of the paschal lamb, that his crucifixion was a punishment for the sins of the world, and made all believers safe for eternity.

This doctrine is one of the most pernicious that has ever been preached. It has been the cause of more crime in Christendom than any other of the teachings of Christianity. The idea that any individual, or deity, suffered for us, and that, no matter what we do, we can solely by faith be absolved from our sins and shortcomings, is too ludicrous to require much consideration. It was born in ignorance and flourished in ignorance, and those who still preach it today are as stupid as those who preceded them.

Fortunately this belief is dying a natural death, and is being hastened to its grave by the teachings of Spiritualism. We know now, from what we are told by those who have preceded us into the etheric world, that each one of us has to bear the consequences of his own sins and shortcomings, and that as we sow, so shall we reap. If we live selfish, evil lives, we shall reap our reward, not only here but hereafter, until we change. The idea of a fixed place for the unbelievers is a myth. We create or own heaven and our own hell. The selfish and wicked are perhaps miserable in the next, though not necessarily. The good and the unselfish in this world may be happy here, and may be happier hereafter. We know now the reason and how simple it all is.

Our mind conditions our surroundings here to a certain extent, but to a much greater degree in the etheric world. If our mind here is self-centred, making us selfish, if it cares nothing for the feelings of others and only for itself, it will create an isolated condition for itself in the etheric world. Through the power of mind we mould our surroundings to a much greater extent there than here, and, as we think, so we are.

It is not difficult to imagine a wicked individual here surrounding himself with equally wicked fellow beings. In the etheric world like draws to like to an even greater extent than here, and consequently evil-doers congregate together.

Just as it is with the wicked, so it is with the good, but there is no great gulf fixed between the two, as the next world is not only a place but a condition. Those who make for themselves evil conditions have always the power of changing them by their thoughts, of thus improving their conditions, and ultimately having harmonious relations with the good. There we get into closer harmony with our desires than we can here. Many a bad individual on earth can cloak his wickedness by his wealth and bluff, but not so there. Our character there is more transparent, whereas here it is not so.

All men and women who have passed from this world to the next have found their level. They may have been kings or queens, princes or lords, looked up to and honoured on earth because of their worldly position, but there, character only determines their position. There they live in a world of finer matter which is more easily influenced by mind, and naturally they gravitate to the surroundings which their minds can best influence. It would be quite impossible there, where only minds in tune harmonize together, for the wicked and the good to live together. They naturally repel each other. It is all very similar to the conditions on earth. There, as here, 'birds of a feather flock together', but, as character is more transparent there than here, one is summed up at once without mistake.

Each one of us is responsible for his own actions and thoughts. Our mental make-up determines our condition hereafter, and no one need be deluded by the idea that belief in some vicarious atonement is going to alter the position each mind determines for itself...

In 1964, Findlay gave one of his beloved country homes, Stansted Hall in Essex, to the Spiritualists' National Union, to be used as a college for the furtherance of Spiritualism and the advancement of psychic science.

He was going to live there too, in a small suite of rooms, but he was taken ill and passed to spirit before being able to take up residence.

The SNU did as Arthur Findlay requested, and named the Hall The Arthur Findlay College. It is today host to students from all over the world, 50 weeks of the year. (Two weeks are given over to repairs and special cleaning, etc. by volunteers from the Spiritualists' National Union.)

Arthur Findlay was also the benefactor who came to the rescue of the now world-famous and long-established Spiritualist newspaper, *Psychic News*, very shortly after it was founded in 1932 when it was experiencing cash flow problems.

MAURICE BARBANELL

The founding editor of *Psychic News* was one Maurice Barbanell. Probably the most famous collection of philosophical work of all is that spoken by his Guide.

Maurice Barbanell himself, like Arthur Findlay, was an accomplished writer and erudite speaker on behalf of Spiritualism, and naturally was more than able to expound on Spiritualism at the public meetings convened for that purpose. He was also a doughty soap box orator at Speaker's Corner in London's Hyde Park, where he would bandy words with hecklers and interested parties alike.

Maurice was the son of Jewish immigrants to Britain, who grew up in the East End of London with a religious mother and an atheist father, neither of whom could resist arguing their point, so young Maurice was given plenty to think about.

It was on the second occasion that he visited a neighbour's flat where the medium was Mrs Bauerstein, that his mediumship was discovered. Maurice only remembers the first few minutes after he and the friend who'd invited him along went inside. He woke up and started to apologize for going to sleep, when the others present told him that he'd been 'used' as a mouthpiece for a highly evolved being in spirit.

That Higher Being was Silver Birch, and he was to speak through Maurice Barbanell, offering much fascinating and thought-provoking philosophy, until Maurice himself passed over in 1981 at the age of 79.

Silver Birch spoke of the power of the spirit in one of his addresses, thus:

The spirit which breathed life into us has given us a common link, because throughout the whole world all the children of the Great Spirit are fundamentally united. The spirit that enables them to live on earth and beyond is the same spirit that makes them a vast family with a common, Divine parent.

It is this sublime truth we seek to express because it is greater than all physical differences, obstacles and barriers. It transcends all colour, language and nationality. It reveals that behind the surface of physical being, there is a common spiritual attribute that binds all people together with an unbreakable brotherhood and sisterhood.

When it is appreciated, it will help to end all war, it will destroy selfishness, greed and vested interest that are far too dominant in many lands. It will substitute the only true superiority, the advance of the spirit over the lower, debased material standards that are far too prevalent.

As this understanding spreads, so the infinite power of the spirit, with all its wealth, splendour, grandeur, love, guidance and healing will manifest in fuller measure and drive out the darkness of ignorance, prejudice and superstition that have reigned for too long and brought chaos and disaster in their train.

You are the Great Spirit in miniature. That power can grow, expand, unfold, enlarge, flourish, bloom, as you allow it to do so. You determined its growth, none else can do it for you; that is the purpose of earthly life. Realize that you are the Great Spirit and you realize that the kingdom of heaven is within you. It cannot fail.

You cannot want, you cannot go hungry, or thirsty once you have adjusted yourself to the laws of eternal supply. You will not receive more than is necessary, but you will receive according to your growth, no more, no less, no higher, no lower.

It cannot be any other way.

PRINCIPLES OF SPIRITUALISM

Spirit is not subjected to the limitations of matter. Spirit, which provides the dynamic of all life, the mainspring of all existence, will provide you with all that you require in your earthly life. The purpose of your being here is a very simple one. it is to fortify, to equip, to unfold that spiritual nature which is yours, so that you are prepared for the next stage beyond death. Thus, every experience, good or bad, sunshine and shadow, strength and weakness, love and hate, health and sickness, adds its quota to your spiritual growth.

There are millions of ways of expressing truth, because truth is of the Great Spirit and it can only be expressed according to the evolution of the individual through whom it has to be expressed. It is through simplicity that you learn truth. Using long words and finding new names does not make for truth. Often, they serve as masks for ignorance.

The truth that we teach is the truth of the Great Spirit that knows no bounds and no limitations. It is for all, not for one. It seeks to embrace the whole of humanity within its loving embrace...

URSULA ROBERTS

Another pioneering Spiritualist medium was Ursula Roberts, whose Guide was Ramadahn, and who was also able to make tapes and have his words transcribed into book form for the benefit of those who would seek to know some more of the multifaceted aspects that are to be found within the philosophy of Spiritualism.

Ursula was also a great teaching medium who didn't mind utilizing her wonderful gifts to help those just beginning to explore and develop their psychic potential.

I am privileged to have spoken not just with Ms Roberts, but with her Guide, and I still remember every word that was said

to me. It was a very long time ago now, when I was just start-
ing out in developing my own mediumship.

Ms Roberts would allow novice students to have access
to Ramadahn through her, and in this way was a great help to
their understanding of the way in which spirit works, as well
as assisting the students' mediumistic progress.

THE QUESTION OF REINCARNATION

One of the most common questions asked of those in spirit is
about reincarnation. The idea of one spirit inhabiting a succession of earthly bodies, one person living more than one lifetime, and progressing through successive experiences on the
earth plane is a concept as old as life itself.

Here again there are various groups within the framework of
Spiritualism who have differing views and opinions about this
possibility.

One of the most fascinating aspects of reincarnation theory
is the wide variety of spirit information on the subject. Some
Guides and helpers have even been known to refuse to be
drawn on it when approached. So the obvious conclusion must
be that it is a subject of some depth and importance, and
should not therefore be dismissed without thought.

National Spiritualism as propounded by the Spiritualists'
National Union does not express a belief in reincarnation. The
SNU has a policy of supporting only the proven and provable
fact of survival after physical death.

As far as the SNU is concerned, reincarnation remains a
hypothetical phenomenon.

Having said that, there are many of its members, and people
among its committees and officials, as well as ministers, who
must believe that reincarnation is a fact. At least two of their
ministers are qualified hypnotherapists who use what is called

'regression therapy' on patients. This is where the subject of the treatment is 'regressed', taken back, to a 'past life'.

One school of thought favours a mediumistic explanation, that people in the spirit world impress themselves very vividly on the minds of those in a hypnotic state of consciousness, transmitting such detailed information about themselves and their own former lives here on earth that the recipient believes that they are truly 're-living' those experiences first hand – and in the first person.

Another theory considers that the earthly existence of one lifespan is not enough for one person to learn their spiritual lesson, and therefore they need to come back and make good what they have fallen short of in order to progress their soul.

Other strands of thought encompass the laws of cause and effect, often referred to by the Eastern word 'Karma', and put forward the idea that if you err in one life, you come back in another body to learn further lessons and overcome new challenges, ostensibly to enable your spirit or soul to journey on to higher things.

Although some Guides are reserved about this endlessly debated subject within Spiritualist groupings, many have spoken, and here is one of such deliberations given from the world of spirit from the group with which I work:

You are asking about the return of an individual's spirit or soul into another body. We who are of the higher realms, the upper dimensions, are often asked about this possibility.

The answer is not always palatable as there are two camps of thought since time immemorial on the earth plane.

Spirit does exist before birth, and enters the physical being soon after conception.

The spirit comes from various dimensions and planes of other existence.

Some it is true are of a simple nature – and some of an extra-ordinarily complex arrangement of mental, mind, abilities, but even at the most 'simple' end of the spectrum, the spirit is able to project vast equations and feats of mental arithmetic that equal the puny efforts of humankind's most exemplary scientists involved in exploration of outer space.

The most simple spirit can work out the space time distance speed and angle of trajectory in order to catch a ball (given the physical mechanisms are also in order). Just a minor example.

The followers and teachers of the 'Mormon' philosophy with respect to their veneration of the past family – similar to the Chinese, and American 'Indians', who literally worship their ancestors and lineage (demonstrated in European context by an unfortunate snobbery) are closest to our own reality, that each individual spirit that inhabits the provided physical frame, remains unique to itself and in relation to its peers forebears and siblings.

There are some who over an eternity of time may return in an earthly form, but this is an exception and not a rule.

This fact has been known to incarnated spirit since the beginning, giving rise to the legend of Messiahs ... and also to spurious claims by misguided human beings to have inhabited the frames of Cleopatra, Julius Caesar, or Attila the Hun!

It would seem easy for those with a simple faith to master life's highways and byways, all the rocky outcrops and pitfalls on the road. For others, the path is never made easy, so that by trial and error and subsequent triumph you might learn the best lessons and so progress your soul.

It is said that some return to the earth plane in order to 'retake their exams' as we might have to return to school for an extra term or two before we can truly leave it behind, tests passed, scholarship attained, but there are others who must learn in one lifespan, all that earth life has to offer.

PRINCIPLES OF SPIRITUALISM

God is ever present as a light – without God there would be nothing but an all consuming evil which would eventually destroy itself.

There are other opposite forces at work in this world and we have a fight on our hands to rid our world of it – first we rid this world and then as a direct result, the next.

God does not punish us for the errors we make, we do that ourselves by suffering the consequences.

There are times, when like any good parent, God stands back to let us make those errors in order that we may learn and grow.

But we are always in the sight of God's good angels, and often those of our family who love us that have gone before to the higher realms.

So for our suffering we must thank God, for our lessons learnt, we thank God also. For the love we experience and the love we receive from fellow human beings we must thank God – also for the hatred we encounter, because we are given an opportunity to turn that hate around, to convince an adversary of the error of their ways, by putting love or at least affection in its place.

Thus we grow and our soul expands.

One thing is an absolute necessity for the enquirer into all aspects of Spiritualism, and that is an open mind.

SPIRITUALIST MEDIUMSHIP: WHAT IS IT?

Mediumship is practised by mediums. A medium is described by the *Oxford Concise Dictionary* as being the intervening substance through which impressions are conveyed to senses. It is an agency or means, and a point between two extremes.

Following on from this, another dictionary definition is that a medium is a person claiming to have communication with the spirits of the dead in order to reveal the results of this communication to others.

In the Spiritualist context, a medium – who is also often referred to as a sensitive – is someone who is the link between heaven and earth, the next world and this, and a Spiritualist medium would be expected to use his or her ability to bring evidence of a loved one's survival and continuing existence after they have died their physical death, in order to comfort the bereaved.

On a less basic level, a medium should be expected to aspire to bring advice and guidance to those still living on the earth plane, and to bring the teachings of rather more exalted beings through to those who wish to hear them.

It is generally agreed among Spiritualists that mediumship falls into two categories, physical and mental. Within these descriptions are many different aspects, each demonstrating particular characteristics.

As we know, modern Spiritualism was founded on contact made through the physical side of mediumship. This required then, as it does now, direction from disembodied spirit intelligence, and the psychic sensitivity of a medium on the earth plane.

This particular kind of obvious phenomena serves to convince even the most sceptical observer that there is more to life than just the here and now. Anyone who has heard or experienced a psychic rap in answer to a vocalized or even a silently thought question, would agree with this.

There is no doubt, though, that this kind of manifestation must be operating completely within the laws of natural science, and therefore would not require any ethical, or religious, commitment from those present at, or involved in, such a display of spirit communication.

To appreciate the significance of this is to understand the implications of another fact of the connecting link between the world of spirit and this world of physical matter: like attracts like. This is a critical factor in 'mental mediumship' as it is called.

A medium has to have a good psychic ability, but someone with good psychic ability isn't necessarily a medium. After all, a medium has to heighten their awareness to a pitch, and tune in to a level where communication from the spirit world, which exists on a much finer frequency than our own, is able to take place.

HOW IS IT DEVELOPED?

Everyone is psychic to a greater or lesser degree.

The vital spark that animates us isn't just linked to the average five senses, but is definitely connected to the sixth, our earthly intuition, sometimes called our extra sensory perceptiveness or ESP.

A PSYCHIC IS NOT NECESSARILY A MEDIUM

A psychic uses this intuition to 'read' body language, which includes facial expression, what the clothes a person wears 'say' about that person, as well as the electromagnetic and emanating energy fields around others known as auras. By linking in to the material energies of the world around them, psychics can gather relayable information about someone's life. And given that information, psychics can not only make some quite accurate assessments of an individual's emotions, state of health and past and present state of affairs, but can also project some possibilities about the outcome of future events. It has to be said that this is invariably a misleading practice given the scientific laws of probability. Psychics who work in this way have not developed their abilities to enable themselves to tune in to the spirit world, but they may sometimes have a clairvoyant capacity which would lead someone who was asking them for advice to believe that they were actually a medium.

TRUE MEDIUMS

Now a medium, like the psychic, is naturally sensitive to energies which may go unheeded by the majority, but a desire to transcend the mundane spurs the would-be medium, who through undertaking much meditation and training learns to identify emanations coming from the discarnate dimension – the world of spirit.

As mediums develop this talent they become aware of the distinctive vibrations separating and distinguishing their helpers, sometimes called Guides, and they also learn how to control and use their faculties to become a good and clear channel for other discarnates in spirit who are existing on other planes.

One of the most important aspects in the development of mediumship is to be able to differentiate between gut response or psychic intuition, and a positive link with a spirit communicator.

As that mediumship develops, so the functions for which the medium is used as an instrument will become known. These are many and various: Clairsentience, which is to be able to feel spirit; Clairvoyance, which means clear seeing; Clairaudience, which is to hear spirit; Inspiration, becoming inspired by spirit; and Knowing, which is to be impressed by spirit.

We are all physically sentient beings first and foremost in our earthly existence. The body that encases us – who are of spirit, coming from spirit and are individual spirit – is tuned in to, and suitable to live amid the gross matter of the physical universe as we experience it in the flesh, here and now.

This sentient framework, our physical body, is very often the first point of contact that those who wish to contact us from the spirit realms are able to reach. It is certainly also key to the physical side of mediumship.

Linking with spirit in this way does not require any intellectual, or necessarily conscious, effort on the part of the medium.

It's a very simple way too, for those in spirit who wish to communicate with loved ones this side of the veil, literally to make their presence felt.

It can be an extremely trustworthy device for giving evidence of survival through someone's trained mediumistic faculty – by transmitting the remembered physical symptoms suffered by the individual in spirit immediately prior to their passing over!

Mediums who use this method for establishing the identity of a communicant, 'die' as many times as they have recipients for their spirit message-givers. However, they don't suffer any lasting ill-effects!

Mediumship itself is often called 'clairvoyance', which in Spiritualistic circles does not mean 'seeing into the future' either, but seeing the world of spirit – or at least relevant parts of it.

Clairvoyance is the ability to see through the dense vibrations of the earth plane, to that ethereal dimension of pure spirit life.

If we understand that all the layers contain consciousness, that the different multitude of planes of life are co-existent at the same time, it becomes easier to comprehend the possibility of a clairvoyant piercing the spatial conditions that prevail at a presently unquantifiable distance from us, using a heightened and psychically developed awareness of our own spirit capabilities.

Clairvoyance actually operates on the same mind frequency that our brain uses for visual imagining. That's why there is an all-important quantum leap to be made from the imaginary to the real during the learning process of clairvoyant mediumship.

A clairvoyant sees those in spirit, and other landscapes and situations, as they are presented, both subjectively – as though watching a television screen (sometimes one with awful reception . . .) and objectively, as three-dimensional depictions in our own earthly space.

CLAIRAUDIENCE

A clairaudient is able to hear those residing in other dimensions, although similarly clairaudients may receive the transmitted information subjectively – through their etheric body system impressed on their inner listening ear – or objectively – as an externally heard physical vocalization.

THE ETHERIC BODY

Our etheric body is the duplicate of our physical self, and is the one by which we are recognized, and made recognizable, by those who are already inhabiting the etheric planes of existence in the spirit world.

The etheric body is, however, as its name implies, of the finer material needed for our continued existence in the etheric (or much more quickly vibrating) planes of spirit life.

The word clairaudience means simply 'clear hearing', although there are occasions when a medium may not be able to hear as clearly as he or she would like.

THE RIGHT CONDITIONS

The congregation at a Spiritualist church or centre gathered for a Divine Service are just as likely to be asked to give their love and kind thoughts to the medium taking that service, as the audience at a secular demonstration of mediumship held in a large theatre.

There is good reason for this apparently altruistically-motivated request.

It is possible for mediums to work under any manner of adverse conditions, but if you take into account the fact that telesthaesic communication is taking place between someone who is spirit still in his or her physical body, on behalf of others in the same condition, and individuals who are in spirit only, via specific mind frequencies, then if there are any negative thought waves from those here on the earth plane, in close proximity to the medium, they can actually cause quite bad interference on the psychic level.

For the clairaudient this can cause them to hear only parts of the messages being sent through to the loved ones and friends who are waiting to hear. So it isn't just the medium who suffers from such antagonistic mind games, but the recipients – and those on the other side of life who are trying to make contact. (For the clairvoyant the result of these hostile signals can be likened to attempting to drive through a blizzard).

Another manifestation of the fact that we all belong to two worlds is the conjunction of our two body forms, that of the spirit and of the material, both clothing our soul.

As we have a physical brain, so we have an etheric duplicate – and we possess a mind which is not of the physical either.

Therefore it has been possible for some people to access their own subconscious both in its physical sense and equally as spirit only. It's the connection between these two worlds that becomes the channel for inspiration from the realms of spirit life.

When the ordinarily conscious mind of the medium has drawn on information pumped up from the medium's own subconscious, which has in turn been given information from spirit via its etheric duplicate, the medium is then able to 'give off', or relay, inspired information.

AN INSPIRED ADDRESS

A medium who serves the Spiritualist churches and meeting places to demonstrate a particular type of mediumship and provide evidence of survival is expected as a matter of course also to be able to give an inspired address – a talk given without notes or prior rehearsal, usually of a philosophical nature and, in churches affiliated to the Spiritualists' National Union, one appertaining to the Seven Principles.

It's perhaps interesting to note that the SNU's education department does advise newcomers to prepare their address in advance. Even so, it's understood that spirit helpers may inspirationally cause the content to vary during the course of its

delivery. The subconscious levels of a medium's mind also supply the impetus for the output of the kind of information from spirit that is termed 'knowing'.

The after-effects of this special variety of mediumship are marked by the medium, who will tell you – 'I don't know where all that stuff came from that was totally accepted by the recipient – I just seemed to "know" it.'

In fact it was channelled from the medium's etheric subconscious, into their physical subconscious, and sweeping past their conscious mind, made its successful spirit world-prompted thought transference, to a hopefully grateful beneficiary.

In this way, mediums are able to receive communication direct from a spirit source, which they then write down without pause or overall comprehension. When this writing is finished, and read back, it often contains philosophical teachings, poetry and spiritual instruction which would not have otherwise occurred to the medium's mind. These writings do need to be properly assessed, to ensure that the source is in fact discarnate spirit, thus adding to the weight of evidence for the survival of individual intelligence, as well as the more general enhancement and advancement of knowledge.

AUTOMATIC WRITING

Automatic writing is somewhat different in essence, as the medium's writing hand moves seemingly of its own volition, but in reality is driven by a spirit communicator and operator.

This method of contact has been used fruitfully not just by those most suited by disposition both mediumistically and those so attuned to transmitting thought in that style in spirit, but by a group of Spiritualist researchers as each of their number passed over to the spirit side.

Those in spirit wrote letters conversing with each other and those on the earth plane, through different mediums who wrote out each individual's words independently. Read on their own they didn't make a lot of sense, and appeared unfinished. Thereafter, when members of the group compared these spirit-dictated and -controlled missives, and read them all together, they made perfect sense.

The Society for Psychical Research (not a Spiritualist organization, but one that has always had some Spiritualists in its number) undertook serious investigation into this phenomena, and has a great deal of archive material on it.

This is called 'cross correspondence', for obvious reasons. As a party game without benefit of discarnate spirit input, it is known as 'Consequences', with each participant writing a line or two on a sheet of paper, folding it over to obscure the words, and passing it on to the next person.

After everyone has had a go, the entire script is read out, usually to hilarious effect. When spirit makes contact using this operational mode, the consequences are most profound, in more ways than one.

In one case, cited by Alice Johnson, the then Society for Psychical Research Officer, a son wrote through one medium, a Ms Forbes, and after giving only part of his message, said he would find another medium who could write 'automatically'. This he did, and completed his letter through a Ms Verrall, which when read by his mother not only made complete sense but was extremely evidential (that is, provided evidence of his survival in spirit).

In this way he had been able to prove his survival after death.

As Arthur Findlay says in his commentary on religious beliefs, *The Psychic Stream*,

> What is today called inspirational, or automatic, writing was considered at the time of the Apostolic Church to come from

God, and that is how the early Christians thought Hebrew prophets, and the apostles, wrote the scriptures. After the canon was decided in 397, the Church announced that inspiration ceased with the Apostles and that all inspiration now rested in the Church, which was guided by the Holy Spirit to interpret the scriptures as God intended them to be understood.

Of course we as Spiritualists attribute life in all its facets as emanating from God as the Universal Spirit and Great Good, and accept that as the supreme progenitor, inspiration – as then all else – springs from that source. However, most of us would accept that our inspiration is received from rather further down the line. But that does not invalidate the outcome.

Where automatic writing is best produced through an uncluttered conduit, for instance as in a light sleep state of unawareness, inspirational communication which requires writing down can be received in a more conscious inner atmosphere.

The sensing, seeing and hearing of spirit emissions are also registered by the medium, who is in an altered state of consciousness to the norm.

But all these mediumistic disciplines have to be transmitted through the receiver's own energy field, spiritual and temporal, and this is where some communication difficulties may be encountered.

This energy field is commonly known as the 'aura'.

THE AURA

The aura is not an abstract mystical concept, but layers of physical electro-magnetism interwoven with etheric substance, the existence of which can be physically established by a photographic method, as well as clairvoyantly perceived by a trained medium. Multi-coloured Kirlian photography is now in the public domain, and Kirlian photographers, who often offer psychic readings as an accompaniment, are generally to be found quite easily at psychic fairs and the like.

The inventor of the technique of passing a high-voltage discharge between the subject and an electrode, which revealed the energy field around the object being photographed, was one Semyon Kirlian in 1939.

The colours emanating throughout the aura are of course vibrating frequencies of light, and although we know that there is light, and therefore colour, hidden from our eyes, below red and above violet, we normally have to make do with the perception of our earthly rainbow!

The seven colours of the rainbow are presented in as many shades as there are frequency changes; from more than 430 trillion vibrations or 760 nanometres at infra red, to 640 trillion and 470 nanometres at mid-blue, to about 700 trillion or 380 nanometres, as violet enters the ultra-violet zone. Through the vibration of light we are actually able to measure and comprehend at least a part of the infinite, and if a part of anything can be found to exist, even though we are unable to find the rest with the present means at our disposal, it must exist within an entirety. Science also tells us that matter which vibrates more quickly contains greater energy than that which vibrates slowly. From our understanding that our material cosmos vibrates with different energies it is only a small step to a general acceptance of both a seen and unseen universe governed by the natural law of still-undiscovered scientific principles.

But again, we can't see subtle differences in shading with our physical sight. Here clairvoyance, along with all the other mediumistic skills, can tell us more.

So what can be discovered about ourselves by the examination of an aura? And, as almost everything we are born with has a function – what is that of the auric field, in mediumship?

You could say it is the means by which thought and sensation from the world of spirit, the etheric universe, are conveyed.

Our inner aura emanates from our core, and spreads out about 2 inches, or 5 centimetres, outside our body. Its form and colour indicate our state of health, while that part of the aura which contains and is regulated by information about our emotional and mental condition normally extends around 2 feet, or about 60 cm, around us.

A medium who is of average intelligence and has a fairly uncomplicated thought process will possess an aura that forms no real barrier to any spirit communication. A complex thought system produces a denser auric field around the intellectual, and is therefore less easily accessed by 'ordinary' spirit.

PSYCHIC ARTISTS

It can be quite interesting and enjoyable either to have a Kirlian photograph taken, or a hand-drawn colour portrait (called an auragraphy) done by a clairvoyant, with a subsequent reading from a psychic who is also a medium taken from either image.

All your life experience is embedded in your aura, including every physical, mental and emotional aspect, and within that, everyone you have ever interacted with.

Therefore a good aura reading can certainly offer you some deep insights into your self – and even some possibilities of future avenues you might like to explore.

It doesn't, however, customarily offer evidence of survival in spirit of your friends and loved ones, unless someone more earth plane-orientated in spirit takes the opportunity to link into an available frequency channel opened inadvertently or deliberately by the auric reader while you are being given this other information.

Pictorial evidence of survival is, however, usually provided by mediums who practise psychic art, which is the drawing or painting of a figurative likeness of someone usually dwelling in the spirit world. There are rare occasions when someone still here in the physical world is intensely troubled, or suffering in some way, causing a concerned loved one in the realms of spirit to impress the troubled person's features, rather than their own, on the mind of the artist.

Thus the recipient of such a portrait, coupled of course with a message, will understand that at the very least help and support from those in spirit who love them is near at hand.

There are many different methods by which spirit works through those who undertake to assist spirit communication in this visual way.

In much the same way that mediums receive automatic writing, some psychic artists, who of course are also 'mental' mediums, allow spirit to control their hand while they hold the drawing tool on the paper, board or canvas. Others enter a deep trance state in order for spirit operators to draw directly through their physical faculties while they are 'asleep'.

Most are in a conscious but mentally receptive condition for spirit side input, and on receiving the visual impressions in their 'mind's eye' are able to copy them down, in just the same way as a regular portrait artist draws from a sitter or model.

PHYSICAL MEDIUMSHIP

As mentioned earlier, mediumship commonly falls into two categories – mental or physical, depending on the type of phenomena being demonstrated or displayed by those instruments of spirit, the mediums. As with the energy frequencies on which all of existence operates, these are overlapping and merging areas.

However, it's generally accepted that physical mediumship provides objectively perceivable evidence of both the reality of the multi-dimensional spirit realm intermingled with this one, and proof of survival after the physical transition called death.

Modern Spiritualism was of course initiated by the physical phenomenon of raps and bangs issuing from that other world, made possible by the necessary mediumistic propensity of those present here on the earth plane, at the right time, and in the chosen place.

As it was then, in 1848, so it is now, and for any communication to manifest between what we often call, for simplicity's sake, the two worlds, there has to be a desire emanating from the spirit side for such to occur, and a psychically developed medium on this side of life.

In order to produce the particular kind of spirit-projected phenomena which can be witnessed by anyone present, a medium with the appropriate assets is required.

There is a natural barrier between this physical world and the world of spirit, and it is this intangible that has to be penetrated for connection to be made between them.

The known physical laws of the material universe that apply to our earthly state, such as those of gravity, the speed of light and sound, the passage of time and measurement of distance, do not apply to the spirit only dimension, and have to be overcome by those in spirit who wish to provide those still living in the physical world with irrefutable proof of their existence, to substantiate the fact of everlasting life as a natural progression to even the most sceptical and physical life-centred individual.

A recurrent feature of almost all physical phenomena is a substance we call ectoplasm.

ECTOPLASM

Ectoplasm is produced from a material that is to be found in the gross matter of the human body, and is used by spirit operators – it must be added, at the express wish of the medium concerned – that when mixed with spirit-side essences provides the means of the physical exhibition of living spirit.

Ectoplasm is most usually associated with the materialization of people from spirit in the seance room, and of course that is an important aspect of its use.

It's fascinating to note that the use of ectoplasmic matter has so far been limited either to altogether lightless, or 'dark room', conditions – bearing in mind that there is 'light' in our earthly darkness that we cannot perceive. Further to that, and still looking at a photographic analogy for a moment, silver darkens when exposed to light – this is the basis of the photographic process in the first instance – but it also darkens in the blacked-out seance room, and even outside of it when mediums work in the ordinary way. For example, if a room is used consistently for sittings by a practitioner of mental mediumship, the fabrics and furnishings of that room will fade at a much faster rate than normal; so, therefore, there is in any case a constant utilization of our physical environment, whether within our individual physical framework, or our outside surroundings, by spirit co-operators.

To get back to the materialization of people from the other side of life, this must surely be the most remarkable and attention-grabbing evidence of survival of all.

The discarnate individual uses the ectoplasm – which flows out from the body of a willing medium while they are in a condition of consciousness called trance – to establish a temporary three-dimensional replica of their own, previously discarded, physical body.

The spirit figure is linked to the medium by a cord – unsurprisingly like an umbilical cord – and is enabled by the power of thought to take on many different shapes, and to produce representations of themselves as they were at various times in their earth life, perhaps as a child, then a mature adult, then in old age.

It has also been noted that while the ectoplasmic figure is moulded by thought, the springboard for all life of any kind, since it is linked physically to the medium it can also be affected by the medium's mind, as well as that of its own and other discarnate spirits who are involved in this very complex process.

There have been some very famous physical mediums who, together with their spirit friends and co-operators, have produced materialized forms of recognizable individuals in front of an audience. Florence Cooke, Helen Duncan and Gordon Higginson are the most well-known exponents, and have now passed over themselves.

Then there is the other use of ectoplasm, ectoplasmic rods. Again, these most frequently manifest in the seance room condition, and therefore have been limited as far as public demonstrations are concerned.

Unfortunately there don't seem to be any known exponents of this sort of physical materialization mediumship at the present time. There are certainly materialized visitations at some seances held in total darkness, when hugs are exchanged, other touches are felt and the occasional cheek is kissed or hand shaken. At one recent meeting, one sitter complained that their foot had been trodden on by someone in spirit who'd walked past them!

These blacked-out seances are conducted for the purposes of a variety of spirit world-induced physical phenomena, using ectoplasm especially, and including 'levitation', 'percussion' and 'direct voice'.

LEVITATION

Although there have been instances of spirit operators levitating (lifting up) the mediums themselves – Daniel Dunglas Hume was seen to rise up several feet from the floor by an

assembly of sitters – the most customarily experienced is the raising, or tilting, of a table.

This is effected by ectoplasm formed into a rod that extends from the body of the medium and that, by means of an ectoplasmic adhesive, is attached to the underneath of the table's top or to its legs.

If the table is too heavy, spirit operators site a lever between it and the floor, to support the weight.

Then, in the darkened room, those sitting round the table recite the alphabet, and the table will be rocked back and forth, or tilted, as specific letters are reached, and in this way words and sentences are constructed that bridge the physical chasm between this world and the next.

If only the psychic energy of the sitters is to be combined with that of the medium to facilitate the movement of the table, along with the spirit-side communicator's directional energies, dialogue *can* take place in broad daylight – or with the lights on.

In this case, as well as the alphabetic method, a basic code of three tilts for yes, two for undecided or doubtful, and one for no, is used.

A bonus at these sittings are raps which may be employed by spirit for spelling words, or answering direct questions, instead of having to tilt the table.

Another manifestation of physical mediumship that has been made available to today's enquirers, is termed 'transfiguration', and is the closest we have to the observable full-figure materializations of old.

TRANSFIGURATION

Again, as before, the modern medium enters a mental condition of trance, so that the spirit operators are able to work undisturbed by the medium's conscious mind. An ectoplasmic

mask is then placed over the medium's own facial features. This is often accompanied by noticeable physiological changes in the size of the medium's hands, feet, hairstyle, etc. This material is a waxy-looking substance that can be viewed quite clearly in a diffused red light. The features of someone living on in the world of spirit, known to one of those who have gathered to participate at such a momentous event, will be impressed on the ectoplasm; recognition is usually immediate. Apart from facial characteristics and expression, when the person in spirit is able to speak the way in which they communicate is in much the same way as when they lived in the physical world, and the information imparted is often of the most intimate nature, known only to the recipient.

My own mother was allowed to contact me in this manner through one of the finest exponents of transfiguration mediumship of our time, Jean Skinner – and it was recorded on video by a gentleman of impeccable antecedents, Ken Britton, who has spent much of his adult life both in the Spiritualist movement and as an investigator of physical and psychic phenomena.

Hardly believing my eyes, I asked, 'Is that really you, mummy?'

The reply, 'You didn't always call me mummy', then a pause, then, 'You once called me "Grumpy"' nearly sent me over to the other side of life myself with shock.

Once, and only once, when I was a very young child, almost half a century before this conversation took place, I had called my mother 'Grumpy Hilda' – and written it on the wall next to my bed!

DIRECT VOICE

The phenomenon of 'direct voice' is also available to interested enquirers, and this is also dependent on psychic energy and ectoplasm, and is therefore demonstrated in the dark.

The ectoplasm of course is supplied by the medium, which can then be manipulated by spirit operators to create an artificial larynx or voice box, through which individuals in spirit can speak; or they can produce a mask, into which the spirit person can push their etheric face to vibrate the air and to enable those present to hear their voice.

In the first stages of direct voice communication, a cardboard or aluminium tube can be provided earth side, as an amplifier, and also as an instrument through which to direct the sound being projected from spirit. This 'trumpet' may be painted with luminous paint, so that it can be seen in the black-out of the physical seance room to very good effect, as it is often to be observed floating around and approaching chosen recipients for communication.

Apport

On the subject of items being moved by spirit, it is possible for objects to be carried through the air, around a room in which people have met to experience some of the physical phenomena of Spiritualist science, and without being touched by any one apparently there. These are known as apports, and they can originate from outside the seance room, from an unknown location.

It has been noted that many apports are given to specific recipients – and even when members of the group change seats, the particular apport follows them.

The personal significance of the gift, and the fact that it is delivered to the right person, clearly shows a motivating spirit intelligence at work.

Throughout direct voice sessions, the medium will be in the condition of unconsciousness known as deep trance, although

on rare occasions the medium has not only remained conscious but has joined in with the conversation between the world of spirit and this one.

SPIRIT PHOTOGRAPHY

It is a medium's human energy that is required when those living in that other world wish to make themselves known through the medium of photographic reproduction. This kind of manifestation into our earthly world is known as spirit photography. Of course, because the entire human race is motivated by and possessed of psychic energies, the appearance of inexplicable spots of light, over exposures, and strange shapes on ordinary family snapshots, are quite common. For this reason they are mostly dismissed as of no consequence, and as the general public is not informed sufficiently about the input of the other side of life into ours, those who have taken photographs displaying such aberrations take it no further.

The fact is that small areas of light showing on photos when they are developed indicate a likelihood of the photographer possessing rather large amounts of the sort of mediumistic psychic potency which, if it were developed, could well produce photographs of people in the spirit realms.

Then there is the reverse possibility, that the person who is having their photograph taken acts as the precipitator for demonstrable spirit activity, having all the necessary psychic components.

There are many different ways in which those individuals existing in other dimensions can impress their likeness on earthly photographic imaging equipment, resulting in a recognizable facsimile of their previous physical appearance.

The main requirement in all cases is a supply of psychic energy and ectoplasm.

It seems almost dismissive of the effort made to utilize these essential ingredients, which together with the power of the fine-tuned thought produces the most amazing pictures, to label them 'spirit extras', but that is the unimaginative tag attached to this phenomenon.

The most famous exponent of this type of spirit photography of all time has to be the aptly named William Hope.

Like most who seem eventually to get drawn in to the Spiritualist way of life, Billy Hope was often made aware of those otherwise unseen people in spirit as a child, and had asked his father at the time to 'send them away'.

Being a spiritually-minded young man, Billy joined the Salvation Army, and one of his own favourite stories of how he came consciously to work for spirit was how he took a picture of one of his friends, and a spirit extra showed up on the photographic plate. As the two looked at it in astonishment, Billy's mate exclaimed, 'Billy, thou art got a dead 'un on t' plate!' It was indeed the likeness of a friend who'd passed over.

Billy then attended a Spiritualist service at a church in Crewe, and afterwards showed this photo to some of the church committee, who not only explained the phenomenon to Billy, but recommended him to a circle where a Ms Buxton was sitting for the development of her mediumship. This began a partnership that was to last 35 years.

When William Hope passed over on 8th March, 1933, he lost no time in making his presence felt thereafter, and only 10 days later appeared as a 'spirit extra' himself on a photograph of John Myers. Thirty years later, a Ms Donnelly in the US received a clear likeness of Billy on a photograph.

As the physical phenomenon of table-tilting can be accomplished using only the psychic energies of the mediums and sitters in ordinary light, so photographs of people living in spirit are produced in much the same way. Spirits project their

own image by a thought process and, enabled by the psychic emanations on this side, also cause a physical reaction on the film, producing what is known as 'thoughtography'.

CONTINUING PROOF OF LIFE AFTER DEATH

Spiritualism's religious, philosophical and scientific principles all depend on the continuing evidential proof of life after death, together with continuous revelation from spirit. To this end, Spiritualism not only needs spiritually-minded people as its adherents, but has to ensure that there are also enough well-trained mediums among its number to serve that specific purpose.

As we are all psychic beings, we all have the potential to develop our intuitive or extra-sensory abilities, but not all will attain the level of skilled mediumship required for public service – whether that be the individual giving of 'private sittings', the taking of Divine Service at church or the holding of demonstrations at centres and meeting place assemblies.

Just as, given the physiological gift of usable hands, we may learn to play the piano, not everyone gets past the preliminary stages or, having done that, becomes a superb musician; so it is with aspirants to mediumship.

Yes, we are all psychic, but mediumship doesn't follow on from that as a natural progression, and just as everyone is born with different potentialities, so it is with both psychism and mediumship.

DEVELOPING MEDIUMISTIC ABILITY

The basic practical requirement for the development of medium-istic ability, is patience.

An appreciation, and recognition, of psychic perceptions is a very important aspect of mediumistic development.

Because mediumship is precisely the exchange whereby the normally unheard and unseen residents in the spirit world are able to communicate in so many wonderful ways with those in our material one, it is essential that other information emanating from that earthly environment does not cause any interference which would result in both a garbled communication, and in doubt being cast on the evidence of survival in spirit offered, therefore undermining the very truth of Spiritualism itself.

Where someone is an adept psychic *and* a medium, this juxtaposition of both attributes can be demonstrated to very good effect through the employment of psychometry.

PSYCHOMETRY

Psychometry can also indicate very clearly how easy it is to confuse the psychic skill with that of mediumship.

An object such as a wedding ring that was worn by someone now in the spirit world, might hold sufficient data about its wearer to convince a recipient who has offered it as a link to a reader on the assumption that he or she is a medium, that actual communication with the ring's owner in the spirit world is taking place.

However, this is what is really happening.

Energy, and its organization (which is the basis of all life, the universe, and everything) is on every level involved with that object. As we know, audio-visual recordings are made by imprinting organized energy information on to specially prepared material which can then be accessed via a pick-up agency.

Everything has psychic energy as a component of its whole, and within that there is an encrypted programme of its existence and therefore a store of information about it; so in the

case of that ring, someone with a fairly well-honed psychic aptitude will be able to pick up and decode this otherwise secret repository of knowledge.

Similarly, because those with psychic talent are able to read other psychically-generated impulses emanating from another human being (some can perform this function with animals too), they can give much information received through their own perception, of a kind that will often astound.

Through reading the auric energy field of an enquirer, the psychic, who 'senses' on the material plane only, may proffer very accurate assessments of their state of health, both emotional and physical, and by noting the past and present happenings in that person's life which are also recorded in their aura, unfortunately will usually make a forecast for the future, although it is only supposition based on the information already gleaned. As a result of the previous accuracies presented to them, there may be a trust put in the predictions that is almost certainly ill-founded.

The psychic, being highly intuitive, will also be able to understand psychological signals, such as nervous gestures, facial expressions, choice of clothes, and so on.

What an enquirer will not get from someone who hasn't moved on to develop their gift any further up the spiritual evolutionary scale to make contact with the etheric and higher realms, is information transmitted from spirit.

Now, a medium who practises psychometry will hold an item that belongs to someone who requires a reading on both levels, and will begin with a psychic reading.

As the psychic awareness usually heightens during the initial stages of the sitting, and the vibrations get quicker and finer, the mediumistic faculty kicks in and the medium, recognizing the change in their own level of consciousness, puts down the object, having attained their link with spirit.

Naturally enough, any who visit a medium who is a practitioner of the psychometric art will take along something that belonged to the person they hope to make contact with, or even a photograph of them, to assist their quest.

In fact the untrained psychic in the same circumstances may well make a connection with the spirit world, but it will be accidental in nature and may be confused with a possible clairvoyant ability on the part of the psychic to 'see' people who have passed to spirit, imprinted on the enquirer's aura, just as they may use that ability to 'view' people and places significant to the sitter by the same method.

In order to transcend the purely material energy generated by the psychic pitch of their work, an aspiring medium must devote much of their own energy to developing a keen sensitivity to the faster and finer vibrational frequencies of spirit emanations.

This development nurtures the sensitivities that must already be present in those who are aware of their psychic abilities, and should be geared towards the attainment, recognition, attunement and control of the mediumistic faculty.

The medium needs first to study their own persona, to know themselves literally inside-out, in order to differentiate between their own self and outside contacts who are not in physical bodies.

A VOYAGE OF SELF-DISCOVERY

This voyage of self discovery, which is of necessity emotionally painful, as well as being a lengthy process, has to take place before anything can be achieved of any real spiritual worth.

Of course, the development of mediumship will proceed in tandem with that inner journey, although in the early stages, self-doubt and concern about what may be being truly perceived, and received, are only the result of an inability to differentiate between what lies within the emergent medium and what without.

As the process of learning starts, one of the most important questions to be asked, when having contact with discarnate beings, is not 'is anybody there?', but 'who is there?'

Because life continues in spirit only as a matter of course, and not as a result of having lived in the physical world as a member of some religious group or belief system, the good and the bad and all degrees between exist in the spirit dimensions, and although Spiritualism avers that soul progress is for all (who desire it), it does mean that identification by the receiving medium is of the essence.

The medium in the early days of development may well be assailed by unpleasant entities trying to gain a foothold of influence back in the physical world, or may be visited by an individual who purports to be someone of importance in human history.

There have also been attempts to impersonate relatives and friends. Bearing this in mind, the injunctions on human beings to love one another and to aim for an ethically decent lifestyle here on earth do not just address the material and physical well-being of the denizens of our planetary incarnation, but our present, and future, welfare as spirit too.

When it comes to accessing the spirit realms, not only does like attract like, the benevolent the benevolent, or the malevolent the malevolent, but those who dwell closest to the earth's dense psychic atmosphere and slower, heavier, vibrations will try and make their presence felt through a good but naive channel.

This is why the simple ouija board, because of the ease by which contact is made for discarnates dwelling on the lower planes of spirit existence, should not be used as a vehicle of communication unless a properly trained medium is present.

The results of haphazard contacts have caused much distress and chaos to those who have taken part in such experiments.

This kind of lower vibrational activity encompasses the possibility of all manner of discreditable discarnates making their presence felt.

When a would-be medium begins to 'sit' for their development, the only impact an individual in spirit calling themselves Jesus, St Francis, Nell Gwynn or Tutankhamen will have is possibly on the ego of the receiving medium; instantaneous flattery, followed by deflation when no definite evidence of identity is given thereafter.

It's possible that the command to 'test the spirits' given in the Bible was for this sort of eventuality. If the personality, intellectual ability or spiritual character is not commensurate with what is commonly known about the individual thus presenting themselves, he or she must be dismissed.

Such are just some of the difficulties that a medium developing his or her abilities for spirit contact may encounter.

Mediums are also called 'sensitives', with very good reason. In order to become a medium for the transmission and reception of earthly and etheric information and communication, their psychic sensitivities have to become even more finely tuned, so that the finer emanations on that much faster, higher frequency of the spirit world can be reached.

Through self-discipline, patience and training, budding mediums learns to control their hyper-sensitivity and to recognize the various levels of awareness on which they are consciously operating.

These levels also include the mediums' earthly surroundings, the conditions prevailing and all the people within their own physical orbit of existence. Not surprisingly, mediums' increased sensitivity makes them particularly susceptible to the usually unfelt emotional emissions sent out as psychic signals

from those around them, and all the other psychically broad-cast vibrations in the environment.

Mediums must be prepared also to develop a positive attitude of mind, to help them overcome what could be rather upsetting revelationary experiences with objectivity and self-control.

As a career move, mediumship is best ignored, but as a vocation, once embarked upon it is indeed a life-changing venture.

Not everyone who wishes to become a medium is able to realize this dream, but there is absolutely no harm in making an attempt, and the first step to the development of mediumship is – the circle.

SPIRITUALIST DEVELOPMENT CIRCLES

The spiritual and harmonious atmosphere that prevails in a Spiritualist development circle room is especially conducive to the well-being of those present.

It is in the safe confines of a pleasant room, usually specially prepared for visitors, that the development of mediumship begins, and can flourish as a consequence.

Development circles, as they are called, can mostly be found taking place in Spiritualist centres and churches as part of their weekly itinerary.

According to the custom of the Spiritualist organization to which the meeting place is affiliated, so it affects the manner in which such circles are constituted and conducted. Some centres require a novice to attend spiritual awareness groups for a length of time before allowing entry into a development circle, while other churches may offer an 'open' circle to all comers, for their initial foray into Spiritualist mediumship.

Then there are 'home' circles, held by dedicated Spiritualists to promote the production of more exponents of communication between the two worlds.

Again, home circles are run in many different formats. The most famous of these operates under one umbrella organization, the Institute of Spiritualist Mediums. Through their 'Home Circle Link' many home circles have over many years been advised and guided on procedure.

It is considered best, however, that before sitting specifically for the unfoldment of mediumship, which should be for approximately one hour, once a week, for however many years becomes necessary, the embryo medium should have undergone a substantial period of preparation.

This should consist of attending awareness groups and classes where psychic exercises are practised and discussed – as well as reading books on every area of the subject. Enquirers after the spiritual truth that rests with their own end goal, mediumship, should also find a discussion group. If there isn't anything suitable available nearby, then they should search out like-minded people to start one, particularly on Spiritualist philosophy.

WHAT ARE THE PHYSICAL MECHANICS OF MEDIUMSHIP?

Meditation is always prescribed as a first step to any kind of communication from spirit, because it primarily trains the mind to shut out the everyday concerns of the physical world.

Of itself, meditation does not necessarily become a conduit for spirit input, rather it can act as a viewfinder and magnifier for what lies within the meditator's own being. It is certainly a powerful tool in the search for self-knowledge, and to that end a meditation group leader who is learned in psychology and mind symbolism, as well as in matters psychic, is of immeasurable value.

The discipline required to sit quietly at a specific time in order to investigate one's innermost being and attune to the

spiritual nature of oneself is a lesson in itself for the hopeful medium. To arrange a time in the physical world to further only hoped-for, eventual contact with the next, is also a lesson in subjugating the importance of earthly life activities in deference to spirit. This is another prerequisite for the Spiritualist medium.

Although a true novice medium's circle is one in which he or she is the single focus of attention, with other Spiritualist members (perhaps church workers) sitting solely for the newcomer's benefit, together with an experienced leader and medium who will be guided and helped by those in spirit assisting in the unfoldment of mediumistic gifts, the other more general Spiritualist development circles also produce good mediums.

As in the single novice circle, so in the other circles; the leader and medium, sometimes one and the same, sometimes not, will observe any changes or signs of spirit working, and will proceed according to the directions given to them by spirit.

In the case of larger circles, containing around six or seven developers, the circle leader may do the 'homework' on behalf of the other members prior to convening, by linking in to spirit for directions beforehand.

This can be done because those who work with us in the spirit world know in advance who will be present, as well as their precise needs at the particular stage of each individual's progression.

In most introductory circles there is some discussion, or at least explanation, of the proposed format, which usually starts with a prayer, possibly a 'round robin', with each participant offering a short spoken thought in turn.

This may be followed by a guided meditation, where the circle leader acts in a similar capacity to that of a tour guide, taking the meditator on a mystery trip, or they might offer just a suggestion in advance of their charge's mental journey.

Occasionally relaxing music may be played as a accompaniment. There are many spiritually uplifting tapes that can be used as a 'sound track' to such excursions of the mind.

One of the functions of spirit-inspired and -guided meditations is to instil discipline (and obedience!) in its followers.

If individuals would rather wander off in a kind of daydream and do what they fancy, rather than follow what are actually firm instructions, however kindly given, they will end up on their own insular road, and not experience the joys of the pathway of spirit. However, those who have volunteered to care for us in that world of spirit have an infinite store of patience for those whose concentration is lacking here on the earth plane, but whose enthusiasm for the attainment of the gifts of spirit are great.

No one is ever abandoned.

'LOST' ABILITIES

There are times throughout mediumistic unfoldment when abilities to see, hear or sense spirit emanations appear to have been lost, but with the trust that is essential the slowly blooming medium will press on regardless.

This is usually the time when other psychic faculties are being worked on by spirit operatives, and once found satisfactory the 'lost' aptitude returns, often improved, together with a new manifestation of mediumship.

Even when all the mediumistic qualities have been explored and all the basic skills acquired, the medium still has to revert back to the very first mode by which contact with spirit was made as they initially sat in the silence of the circle room, before they commence their work of relaying message from loved ones, or teachings and philosophy from the more 'elevated' planes of spirit.

It is in that original circle where they sat for attunement to the vibrations and frequencies of spirit communication that the medium first learned to respond to spirit contact, to identify the various individuals in the spirit realms and the capacity in which they came through – whether as a Guide, helper or door keeper who has become quite familiar, or as an occasional visitor who has fulfilled a specific purpose at that time.

This contact evolves through the harmonious and sympathetic atmosphere generated by a capable circle leader and the sitters present, while the prospective medium tunes in to the conscious frequency level of the spirit world. These are the conditions that allow those in discarnate life to adjust their vibrations – to slow them down, in fact, to facilitate a meeting with the medium incarnate, who has learned the process of speeding up and increasing his or her own vibrations.

WHO CAN BE A
SPIRITUALIST MEDIUM?

Anyone with an awareness of their own psychic perception – used either to using their intuition to interpret situations and circumstances, or having an understanding of the reason behind not taking to some people or places on initial contact, for example – and who has a sincere desire to develop their own mediumship for the benefit of others, to comfort the bereaved, bring spiritual teachings to humankind, expound the truths of Spiritualism and become a link between this world of matter and the world of spirit, will be able to build on their inherent and inherited psychic faculties.

As far as their development will take place, that depends on a variety of factors.

Inherited tendencies are a major determinant, and of course the attitude of mind, personality and spirituality of a novice medium, as well as the quality of the energies available from the other sitters and circle leaders when they join a circle.

Once development is commenced, the student will begin to respond to spirit influence, but the timespan which determines how long it will take before this contact can be relied upon is unpredictable.

UNIVERSAL CRITERIA FOR MEDIUMSHIP

There are many different sorts of circles available for the development of the various kinds of mediumship, but there are basic universal criteria.

The first is to ensure you have a good leader, someone who has a comprehensive knowledge of the subject and the ability to observe analyse and guide circle members. The leader should also be able to demonstrate that they are capable of following the instructions of spirit workers as to the circle programme, and thereby gain the confidence and respect of the students. A student, however, should not carry out any instruction with which they feel uncomfortable, or that is against their own principles.

The presence of a good medium is also extremely advisable for maintaining communication and the co-operation of spirit helpers, and for providing mediumistic insight into the students' – or single student's – current development.

Better still, the proximity of another medium does help the student medium's abilities along. Also beneficial is the services, where possible, of a circle recorder, something like a minutes secretary, who will make notes of all that transpires, including any messages from spirit.

Many now-famous Guides – Silver Birch, for one – first had their teachings transcribed by such a note-taker. And it is thought, through spirit intimation, that there is a spirit world record kept of all that is, and that this is usually called the 'Akashic' record.

Even if the room set aside for a development circle is pleasant enough, and the energy is high and generally conducive to spirit communication, if you, the aspiring medium, feel unhappy with anything, or anyone part of the set-up, then move on and find another circle.

It can take a while for some people to find the right circle for themselves, but spirit is always cognizant of every situation, so there is no need for worry.

As for the circle room itself, it should be clean and airy. The chairs should be straight-backed and the seat at a proper height from the floor. Glasses of fresh water should be available for all the participants.

The room's atmosphere should be like that of a sanctuary, away from the hustle and bustle of ordinary life. The student medium should feel safe to go within the depths of their own mind, and there find the sanctuary of their own inner consciousness, wherein, and whereby, contact with spirit may be made.

This act is achieved by withdrawing mentally from the physical surroundings, and creates the conditions for the sensing and selective tuning to spirit vibrations.

Once the circle is brought to a close, members can discuss the progress of the hour, any interesting results, and maybe have some kind of refreshment like a cup of tea and a biscuit – two items any Spiritualist medium shouldn't be without!

Although there is common ground and ultimately a common purpose to circle work, circles that are convened for different types of development may well have a different 'pack drill'.

THE FOUR TYPES OF CIRCLES

The four main categories are perception, control, healing and physical mediumship.

PERCEPTION CIRCLES

In a beginners' circle, interesting experimental psychic exercises will be performed to increase the student's sensitivities, and these may also lead to linking in to other circle members' auras

58

and giving readings from them. Once the novice medium reaches the point where they become aware of the level of consciousness where those in spirit may be reached, they will then be encouraged to link in to their helpers and get to know them, and on what frequency they come in.

This is the stage when a student medium asks the communicating spirit person, 'What's your name, age, profession, memories, relationship?' and for 'any message' for a recipient in the circle.

CONTROL CIRCLES

Circles that deal with control are not in such plentiful supply, and are usually geared to one person's development only. The leader usually asks the discarnate entity some relevant questions to encourage them to come through the medium. This kind of mediumship can develop into what is known as a full trance state, where a person in spirit speaks through that medium, or it may develop into physical mediumship.

HEALING CIRCLES

Healing circles bring together those whose leaning towards this type of mediumship is spotted in the development class. Although all aspiring mediums should read as much as they can of the philosophy and history of Spiritualism, as well as books that inform about the various aspects of the mechanisms of mediumship, healers should also read up on the ethics of their calling, ensuring that they know the Spiritualist healer's Code of Conduct and information about a healer's legal responsibilities, such as insurance.

Some circles will offer students the opportunity to study other kinds of healing, such as that using crystals, as well as through their own mediumship, healing Guides and helpers.

A physical circle is only ever for one medium's development, and is certainly not an oversubscribed discipline. It is invariably held in the dark using a dark red light as the only source of illumination.

Physical circles are conducted in a similar way to control circles, but here manifestations of spirit presence and influence make themselves felt as 'psychic breezes' – cold draughts, and physical sensations of their solar plexus being pulled – by sitters and student medium alike.

Singing and conversation of a spiritual nature will help to produce and keep up the appropriate level of vibration for the spirit operators. Needless to say, physical mediums are few and far between.

Circles generally are fairly plentiful, and many Spiritualist churches and centres run them and welcome enquiries.

WHERE TO FIND MEDIUMS

Spiritualist churches and centres are not just a source of responsible and reliable mediums developed through their good offices, but are also the places to find good mediums working.

As Spiritualism has no one day earmarked as 'holy' or labelled the 'Sabbath' or specific day of rest, services are held on any day or days throughout the week, whenever has proved convenient to the members.

Because Spiritualism believes in nothing that can't be proved, and is founded on the belief in unconditional life after death, which is made manifest through mediumship, mediumship is in evidence at every meeting.

Most Spiritualist meetings are introduced by a chairperson who welcomes the congregation and then introduces the medium

who will be taking the service. This is usually followed with an inspirational prayer, or invocation, offered by the medium.

As Spiritualism is also a religion, it has elements of praise and worship, and the majority of meetings include reverential and uplifting songs and hymns, although there are some assemblies which are loath to take on board what could be seen as orthodox religious habits.

Occasionally there will be a separate speaker who delivers a discourse around the philosophy of Spiritualism, but more usually the medium who is to supply the 'clairvoyance' for the service, also provides the address.

This section is often followed by information about the church or centre's activities for the week, and any other relevant news, after which the medium is invited to demonstrate their particular type of mediumship.

As this is expected to give those gathered evidence of the survival of their loved ones, it will be of the 'perceptive' type, even if the address owes something to a light state of 'control'.

In this way, a few members of the congregation will receive such proof personally, while everyone else will be content to witness the evidential information publicly tendered.

Most Spiritualist meeting places have those considered 'resident' mediums, who are available to give private sittings, or group readings, at a reasonable cost – most, if not all, of which goes to the church to aid its upkeep.

There are usually set days and times when these services are available, and they are usually mentioned during the reading of church notices during the service, pinned to the church notice board, or advertised in *Psychic News*.

A private sitting is one where an individual enquirer visits the medium, who links in to spirit on their behalf for an agreed amount of time, which can be anything from 15 minutes to one hour. This transpires in private.

A group reading is one where the medium accepts more than one person desirous of hearing from spirit, sitting together in one place and for an aggregate length of time.

It's quite common for about 8 to 10 people to receive information, one after the other, over a period of an hour and a half, with one medium. Most come away feeling quite comforted and satisfied.

Apart from the religious centres, there are the fixed focal points, such as the Arthur Findlay College, where the tutors are known to take bookings for sittings – again, a portion of the fee goes to the College.

Other national organizations such as the Spiritualist Association of Great Britain offer sittings with their approved mediums on a daily basis, and the White Eagle Lodge based in London and in Liss, Hampshire, is also a source of mediumship, although their emphasis is on group meditation.

The Spiritualists' National Union keeps a register of exponents, and *Psychic News* also regularly reports on mediums' activities, and has reliable classified advertisement columns that feature mediums.

The Institute of Spiritualist Mediums may also put prospective enquirers in touch with their registered approved mediums.

IS IT ALL RIGHT TO DISTURB THE DEAD?

Our physical bodies come with an inbuilt basic survival instinct, the desire to keep body and soul together, designed to ensure that on the whole throughout our earthly lives we don't take decisions on behalf of our physical and temporal self, or chances, which would be most likely to separate the one from the other before time.

Even as each lifetime continues onwards through its span of years, and is given the attendant development capacity to contemplate its condition and state, in a thoughtful way, by the individual possessor, the notion of the indivisibility of matter and spirit is almost too strong to dispel.

As a result of this almost immutably entrenched general attitude of mind, the majority of religious sects offer an easily acceptable view of death that is projected as though it were a physical sleeping process, and although it is understood, and promoted, that the physical body decays, these sects aver that the spirit will be reunited with that body and resurrected on a 'day of judgement' – 'when the last trump shall sound' or any number of variations on that theme.

There are many contenders for worst or most spiritually misleading pronouncements on what happens after physical death, probably because of this instinctive inability to acknowledge the independence of spirit. The Humanist believes that the physical self is all there is, and that's that; the Christian believes that you will only live on if you accept Jesus as the Messiah (the other side of that coin is that if you don't, you're damned), the Orthodox Jew believes in resurrection in the same body at a future date set by the Almighty, and the Reformed Jew has moved further towards the Humanist doctrine, changing one of the traditional prayer formats to say thanks for 'giving all life', rather than 'everlasting life'. So really you can take your pick.

Moving further east in global terms, the more 'other worldly' become the pontifications on death. Although many in the West now seeking a more mystical way of looking at life are attracted by certain Eastern religions, some may wish to draw a line, or veil, over the prospect of reincarnation.

Spiritualism states that we live on as conscious but discarnate entities, as our birthright.

Any amount of concrete laid over our dead bodies, large stones or marble mausoleums, will not curtail our spirits, neither will cremation – or burying our remains at crossroads.

When a Spiritualist medium tunes in to the higher vibrational frequencies of the realms in which dwell those who have discarded their physical overcoats, they are merely opening up a channel for communication, in the same way that a radio or television is switched on and tuned to a pre-set wavelength and frequency to receive transmissions. If the radio or television station did not send out specifically directed signals, the listener or viewer couldn't access the programme, however much they wanted to. This is the same principle that operates when mediums pick up messages from the spirit regions.

There have been many attempts throughout the ages, on the part of those in powerful establishment positions threatened by the power of the spirit world, to curtail and even assassinate those who have been in touch with these messages.

This is why there are exhortations against talking to the dead in the Bible, and why even common rumour has it that it's wrong to communicate with those who have passed over. Yet all the great prophets recorded in the Bible were mediums. Jesus himself is reported as having been seen speaking to both Elijah and Moses, wonderful mediums in their own right, and yet the latter, in relaying information from the Guide of Israel (Jahweh) is described as having told the Israelites not to have anything to do with those who were 'wizards' or who had 'familiar spirits'. Familiar spirit, as defined in the *Concise Oxford English Dictionary*, is a 'demon attending and obeying witch, etc.' Now demon in English is an 'evil spirit' – but in the Greek, in which the aforementioned scriptures were actually written, daemon simply means 'supernatural being' or an 'attendant or indwelling spirit'.

In fact it was Deuteronomy, Chapter 18 verses 9–12, 'thou shall not suffer a witch to live, or [anyone] who is a medium or

spiritist or who consults dead', which prevented me from taking any notice of my own contact with spirit. Knowing what I now know, I feel even more deceived personally, and angry too on behalf of the many thousands – and millions as we stretch into the future – who may be as convinced as I was that the way of Spiritualism was wrong, and who may be lost to the truth of Spiritualism.

If those dwelling in the realms of light choose to make contact with us who remain here at the staging post for our time being, we should welcome them as we would any visitor to our earthly home.

One thing I'm sure of, they are not disturbable.

BUT CAN YOU TALK TO A GHOST?

You can talk to a ghost, but you won't get an answer! A ghost is just that – a shadow of someone's former self, or a reproduction of a place, imprinted on the atmosphere. That's why ghosts are often seen at the same place, the same time, performing the same task or going through the same motions.

For instance there are reports of regular enactments of bloody battles, many times actually heard rather than seen, on the sites of previous conflicts; the Civil Wars in England and the US certainly left their ghostly mark.

It may be postulated that everything that has taken place in this world has been recorded either by impression on the planet itself, as a kind of spherical electromagnetic tape machine, or on the atmospheric material that surrounds it. This could possibly account for the large-scale battlefield replays, such as the widely reported event that two tourists experienced in the gardens at the Palace of Versailles, when they suddenly found themselves in an 18th-century environment peopled by courtiers in period dress.

Then there are the ghosts that frequent houses, stately and small, often walking through walls (that weren't there originally) or seen floating above the floor because the old building had different floor levels.

But whether they appear wearing distinctive clothing, or diaphanous robes, they are just ghosts, moving holographic pictures. You might talk to the images on your television screen, but they can't hear you, see you or talk back.

WHERE IS THE SPIRIT WORLD?

The spirit world is all around us, but is not of us. We are of it. It is the heavenly matrix of light, the etheric grid, which supports this physical plane of existence in its entirety. Our universe, our world, is held fast within the interpenetrating web of spirit substance, and as the physical lifespan expires and decay sets in, so the spirit stuff that has supported it begins to function in the solely spirit-compatible environment of the other world.

This 'other world' is part of an eternal universe that is unconstrained by the physical laws of material science, and therefore without gravity or a restrictive speed of light.

Because every physical manifestation is maintained by these unperceivable spirit light-frequencies, whether it possesses a motivating spirit consciousness, as in the human being for example, or whether it was produced as a spiritually inanimate object, such as a house, a car or a woolly vest, an etheric counterpart will exist.

This phenomenon accounts for stories of people who, having departed this life unexpectedly through an accident or other unplanned agency, wander around not understanding their new status, nor realizing that they are, to most people that they see around them, dead.

Nevertheless, few are left to ponder and puzzle for very long, as friends, relatives and other loved ones already in spirit will receive the information that this individual has come over, and rush to welcome them.

Even where someone would assume they had no one to whom they would be significant on the other side, the powers that be will make arrangements for that person's reunion with at least some of their forebears, who of course will be delighted to greet them, introduce themselves and make them feel at home.

There are the odd occasions where some slip through the net, perhaps through the strength of personal choice, for whatever reason, and these are often picked up by 'rescue circles', groups of spiritual philanthropists which contain at least one strongly mediumistic individual and which specialize in getting people to 'move on' from the earth plane to the next.

WHAT IS IT LIKE?

It's this next plane, often called the 'astral', that is described as resembling this one.

Our essential consciousness, the soul, now clothed in our first spirit body, is now further along an eternal route that will ultimately lead to perfection.

It's the soul, containing our mind, the repository and generator of thought, that is considered to be that part of our being that is connected to the universal, or cosmic, subconscious, to which we have little access while we're in the physical plane.

In ordinary physical circumstances, where there is no impairment of the senses, a young child can demonstrate the truth of this statement. An adult may throw a ball to a 4-year-old, who will catch it. That child has had to work out – subconsciously – the trajectory and speed, dependent on thrust and weight, of an object approaching through the air, and work out precisely where they must place their body, and hands, in order to receive the missile.

Those who hypothesize that the brain is everything, and that the mind is the same as the brain, might like to ponder where the algebraic expertise that was needed, coupled with the physical dexterity of the tiny ball catcher, comes from.

Once in the spirit world our own individual memories and subconsciousness are restored to us as full consciousness, a necessary requirement in the pursuit of self-knowledge that enables the soul to progress. Because of this connection between the conscious and subconscious, there is far more control by the individual over their etheric or spirit body.

Sensory capacity, too, is extraordinarily enhanced in the spirit world and, thought being the medium by which all in spirit life is accomplished, speech is transmitted telepathically, no matter the distance, while an individual's vision is not restricted by location either, as it is in the earthly sphere.

The power of thought brings infinite possibilities within the range of those dwelling in the spirit realms. Teletransportation within their own dimension is achieved by mental concentration.

There is still, however, a difficulty in inter-dimensional interaction, as those of us on the earthly plane live in spirit but also in bodies that are suited to the prevailing vibrations. The earth plane is the most dense, the astral plane less dense; the succeeding planes becoming finer and finer.

This is the crux of the problems encountered in communication between those in spirit and those in the here and now. As the spiritual vibrations of the individual in spirit increases, it becomes more and more difficult to have meaningful contact with the denser levels that have been left behind, and almost impossible for communication to transpire between the heavier vibrationary dimensions and those on finer frequencies.

PRINCIPLES OF SPIRITUALISM

Thought shapes and determines our environment in every sense of the word.

While those determined as a first – or even second – requirement of their ascent to life in spirit, to seek spiritual wisdom and have the desire to dwell among higher beings in spirit, will strive to progress through the denser planes of spirit existence, others, reflecting the earthly material conditions, are in the majority, happy to contemplate eternity with their nearest and dearest, in surroundings that they feel comfortable in. All this, of course, depends on how they have lived their lives.

Even so, given the positive spiritual influences that are in evidence all around, there is a slow progression towards desire for elevation of the soul that stirs the spirit. Once it is realized that links are not severed as in physical separations, and that love is the force that binds all irrevocably, those who may have been thus happily amouldering will look to widen their spiritual horizons, and begin to move on.

WHO INHABITS THE SPIRIT WORLD?

For those who have led distinctly unspiritual lives on earth, unpleasant conditions beckon. It is considered generally in Spiritualist terms that these people are left to the companionship of their own kind, and to the reflection of their own evil actions and thoughts.

Living on in such abhorrent conditions, constructed for themselves as they made their wicked way in their earth life, they may become revolted, and so their soul institutes a struggle to free them. Previously imprisoned by low-frequency materialistic impulses, the effort to break out stimulates their spirit and a glimmer of spiritual light becomes apparent.

Many adjustments have to be made and drastic changes undertaken, supervised by more highly evolved beings, before any spiritual progress can be substantiated. For some, and we all have our own list, this process of progress will take an eternity.

There is a great difference between this murky dimension and the 'summerland' wherein many reside after passing to spirit. Surroundings are to be found that are familiar: countryside, towns, rivers, lakes and seas, and even religious buildings, considering that further up the spiritual evolutionary scale sectarianism and adherence to specific religion ceases.

Then there are crystal caves and halls of learning, and places where those more highly evolved in the spirit realms visit, in a guiding and instructing capacity, to assist in the progression of our own aspiring spirit.

There are resting and recuperation sanitaria where those who've suffered trauma in their physical lives can recover before taking up their options.

There are libraries – with all the books that ever were, and entertainment centres which, like the Windmill Theatre during the last World War, never close.

Sleep, and eating and drinking, are naturally unnecessary, although there is a source of etheric food and drink representational of that which is available on earth, and giving a special kind of nourishment to the spirit.

Before my mother passed to spirit after suffering a cancer that prevented her from eating, something she particularly enjoyed, she was given a message from spirit that promised her 'bread and onion soup' on her arrival. My mother told me that she looked forward to that, and I have no reason to doubt that this is what happened and that she enjoyed the meal.

The pioneering Spiritualist medium Ursula Roberts herself mentioned that she was most looking forward to dancing, having endured a disability of her leg after having polio as a child, for all her adult life on the earth plane.

I myself have seen ice rinks, in use, on the other side, and I know that all who wish to experience the thrill of skating, no matter what their physical constraints have been, will be able so to do after they have cast off their physical shell.

I hasten to add that all this in the proper fullness of time.

There are all God's creatures too in the etheric world, and those who have loved animals will not lose the opportunity of continuing to do so. Animals, too, cast off their physical encumbrances and remain in spirit.

It does appear that animals and birds who have enjoyed a relationship with a human being occupy a particular niche in the spirit world, and this has led to a widely held concept that animals and birds who have been pets, or otherwise loved by humans, only enjoy their existence in spirit as a direct result.

I have never subscribed to this notion, and as well there have been many instances of animals and birds making their presence felt via the good offices of a medium, and clairvoyant sightings of cattle and other animals too.

It might be an instance of ghostly impression only – there has been no investigation to my knowledge – but the Market Estate residents in North London used to be awakened regularly by the sound of cattle. Their homes were built on the site of the old cattle market and abattoir. . .

It's interesting to note that after their own passing, many animal lovers opt to care for animals who are in the spirit world, especially those who were pets and are waiting for their human companions to join them once again.

These animals are known to live in very conducive surroundings as befit the innocent, and those who look after them are to be thanked.

Most innocent of all are the children who pass over, and they enjoy special arrangements for their welfare. As they leave the physical world behind, they begin their spiritual progression at exactly the same point.

As children are closer to having experienced their birth into the physical world, birth into the next is not too different an experience, and even for those who for any reason were never 'born' in the physical sense, still have a smattering of knowledge about physical conditions that would make them glad to be existing as spirit alone!

There are guardians to take care of these children, as well as family gone before and their friends, and so on ad infinitum. Therefore no child is ever isolated in spirit.

Their etheric bodies grow as they would have on the earth plane – the etheric body is always a fully working model, even if the physical one doesn't work very well or is incomplete in some way. This etheric body includes the mind, which is obviously, therefore, *not* dependent on the existence of a physical brain, whether in physical working order or not.

Part of their education is to return, as spirit naturally, to what would have been their earthly home, to know a little of earthly joys and affections.

Even in areas of great material deprivation, the children are shown how the spirit transcends and supersedes the physical, and how love still blooms within the soul.

They are sometimes able to communicate with those on the earth plane, particularly family members, and so in this way they are participating in the practical process of spreading the knowledge about immortality that is the basis for Spiritualism. These children, as they grow up in spiritual and harmonious surroundings, delight in helping others and performing other tasks which they know will accelerate their own progress. As they develop their spiritual abilities, these innocents are the teachers and helpers of those with difficulties on the earth plane, or for the spiritually ignorant and unenlightened who pass into the world of spirit in that state.

Not everyone in need requires the help of someone who has experienced it all themselves first-hand.

It ought to be mentioned that some who set out in the usual way of a pregnancy, but are not actually born to live on the earth plane, for whatever reason, are sometimes not intended to be, and these are highly evolved souls assisting, in an esoteric way, the progress of others involved in the course of these events. They live in much more rarefied planes of consciousness and existence.

The other dimensions of graduated finer vibration are the dwelling places of all those who have achieved particular degrees of spiritual evolution. Unlike the physical law that operates on the earth plane, when the material covering of the spirit is shed according to physical wear and tear or accident, regardless of the spiritual attainment at that point by its occupier, those in spirit discard their various etheric coatings only after particular spiritual progress has been made.

The ultimate dimension is that occupied by the Designer of all that was, is and will ever be, the imponderable, and yet not entirely unknowable. Spiritualism teaches that God is everywhere and in everyone, and as we get to know the best of ourselves, our soul and spirit, which is part of the Great Spirit, we will know God.

Then there are the places where angels attend to their duties, the prophets of old – mediums who devoted their earthly lives to the relaying of spiritual knowledge to the earth and who, just like the mediums of the last 150 and more years of modern Spiritualism, have been misquoted and misrepresented by the spoken and written word here and there, as well as other noted people who lived highly spiritual earthly lives.

Then there are those, on the same, or 'higher' levels of spirit, who were unknown except to a few, and some who are even more elevated souls who were completely anonymous in their lifetime.

Many who lived ethically and philanthropically without recourse to, or who were even antagonistic to, religion of any kind, are also known to inhabit the upper reaches of life in spirit, after spending their lives attempting to improve the quality of earthly life for many.

And so you see, as all who have ever been born into this life are still in conscious existence, it only takes a little imagination and thought to know who is likely to be where on the spirit 'ladder'.

IS IT POSSIBLE TO TELL THE FUTURE?

All the signs point to the possibility of foretelling future eventualities; but there are perhaps too many spiritual pitfalls surrounding this possibility to make it an ethical proposition in the general scheme of things. However, there is no doubt, from the evidence of those communicating from the higher realms, that there are at least a few fixed points in any one person's life on earth. These, more than likely one at a time, are vouchsafed uniquely from that higher source, and that for purely intrinsically good reasons.

A Spiritualist medium will usually be the chosen instrument for such highly confidential, and possibly revelationary, information, although many who would not perhaps call themselves mediums, Spiritualist or otherwise, have received this kind of message directly, albeit mostly in the sleep state.

The paths we take towards these points in our lives are our own choice, given free will, and applying, hopefully, a sense of personal responsibility.

In any case we are responsible for our actions. It might be said that it's an abrogation of that responsibility that makes human beings want to know what's going to happen next in their lives – as though they themselves have no part to play, and that they have been provided with a completely charted course, travelling without recognizable references, on autopilot.

Spiritualist mediums are protected now by the Fraudulent Mediums Act of 1951, although I would like to see a change of heading. This act provides for 'the punishment of persons who fraudulently purport to act as Spiritualistic mediums or to exercise powers of telepathy, clairvoyance or other similar powers'.

This statement therefore presupposes and admits in a legal framework that there are, in fact, genuine mediums.

Before this Act, mediums were prosecuted as witches under the Witchcraft Act (which dated from 1735!) for 'attempting to raise the spirits of the dead'.

It says much for the public work of many Spiritualist mediums since 1951, that there is now a growing acceptance of the veracity of Spiritualist mediumship, which demonstrates and confirms communication between spirits living in physical bodies down here, and spirits of the dead living over there.

Whether such interworld communication contains information about the more or less immediate future life of a recipient as well as proof of the communicant's survival, is up to both a Higher Authority, and the integrity of the medium.

Most mentions of this kind of thing are ordinarily about matters of great concern to the recipient, even if they're not earth-shattering in content.

'They say you're going to move home next year,' may sound banal – but if the recipient is living in unacceptable conditions, perhaps with dreadful neighbours or with stairs that are too steep, or any other problem, that message will give great hope, and if it comes from spirit it will come to pass.

Similarly, if a recipient is told that they needn't worry about a specific health condition, or that they are not expected on the other side for a long time yet, it may be that their loved ones in spirit, knowing of their distress, need the medium to pass that message on. This too will result in relief for the recipient – and will increase their conviction about survival for everyone in spirit.

This kind of prognostication is much closer to the prophesying of old than to fortune-telling, which is closer to the reading of signs and interpreting omens, although this practice has continued through time to this day, when it seems to be ever more popular!

Prophecy literally means speaking for God-spirit, whereas fortune-telling has only ever been a psychic exercise, without spirit input, dealing in supposition and paths of probability.

Prophecy has always been a medium's role, and Spiritualism as a religious movement maintains that it is a sacred office and expects its adherents who are mediums to bring teachings from the higher spirit planes for the benefit of humankind.

It was in this capacity that the mediums, the prophets, of the old religions operated.

Spiritualism is a new religion based on old truths that still stand. The new mediums are more openly consulted by people than was recorded before, and although the ancient world had its fair share of the spiritually motivated, the more materialistically-inclined psychics were definitely more popular, as they are still today.

SPIRIT-INSPIRED EVENTS

There are many instances of spirit-inspired psychic events written about and spoken of in every religion on earth. The manifestation of this phenomena is the same now as it ever was.

For example, it is quite possible for those in spirit to impress their image and that of their surroundings on to any surface – and so it is not difficult for a clairvoyant medium to see there 'apparitions', and sometimes intimations of the future, in just

the same way as Joseph – he of the rainbow 'coat of many colours', used his silver cup...

The Bible is full of mediums, prophets and how they relayed information from the spirit realms to those on the earth plane who were living at the dawn of civilization many thousands of years ago.

The messages they received seem strangely at odds with our present-day sensibilities and understanding of how we should live according to Spiritualist values, but these were the early days of recorded history, and involved many groups of people, including one group of people in particular who were subdivided into huge extended families – the tribes of Judah.

The communications that, like every message nowadays, are allowed by God, the Great Creator, were directly attributed thereto, although in the light of modern Spiritualism we understand that they emanated from the various levels of spirit existence.

Nevertheless all the accounts of spirit intimation that was repeated by the – predominantly, it would seem, clairaudient – mediums living on the earth at that time have proved to be correct. As the Bible is full of examples of mediumship it is hard to single out any particular instance, but as an example of messages that speak of the immediate future in a very unspectacular way, Elisha said, 'Hear the word of the Lord. This is what the Lord says: about this time tomorrow, a seah of flour will sell for a shekel, and two seahs of barley for a shekel at the gate of Samaria.'

There had been a siege of the city and prices of food were sky high – a donkey's head costing 80 shekels and a cab of seed pods 5 shekels. As told in Book of Kings, the siege was lifted the night of Elisha's prophecy and there was suddenly a glut of food on the market. The measured quantity of flour sold for a shekel, as did the barley.

The medium who stands on the public platform and offers information, in much the same way now as then, also demonstrates that those who dwell in the spirit dimensions still reveal the truth to those living on the earth, no matter how unspiritual this plane still is.

ETERNAL FUTURE FOR ALL

Spiritualism doesn't offer inexplicable miracles or redemption from sin through a saviour, or an afterlife as a result of accepting specific conditions.

Spiritualism does not consider other philosophies and religious to be any less spiritual, and acknowledges all the selfless and good people who have belonged, or presently belong, to other belief systems.

Spiritualism as a way of life places every emphasis on the fact of an eternal future for all.

Because of this assured collective future that will be spent in the realms of spirit, Spiritualism identifies the common enemy of the spiritual progress and welfare of the earth as materialism.

Spiritualism also demonstrates that although the physical and material are temporal and temporary, soul and spirit are for ever, progressing ever onward through eternity.

Spiritualism is a down-to-earth religion. It has nothing whatever to do with superstitious practices, beliefs or rituals. Instead of 'faith', Spiritualism offers demonstrable knowledge.

Neither does Spiritualism favour prayers learned and repeated by rote. Rather it places emphasis on inspiration from spirit whether offered by a medium or other speaker taking a meeting or service, or as private individual thought or devotions.

Spiritualism has no dogma or creed associated with it.

Nevertheless as a religion it has all the pith and moment of the essential ingredients that are the basis of every other religion.

God is perceived as omnipresent and eternal spirit, with human beings as an individualization of this Great Spirit, and all subject to the natural and unchangeable laws which govern all life.

The Spiritualists' ambition is to live ever more closely and harmoniously to that Supreme Spirit by service to others and helping as many as possible to share in the really good things in life. Participation in social projects as an expression of love and concern is to be actively searched out, as by bettering more people's material lot, spirituality and the tenets of Spiritualism can take precedence over materialistic concerns.

Spreading knowledge about the truths incumbent in eternal life helps towards the eventual time when humankind understands that it is one family in spiritual union, all connected to the One Source.

Spiritualism is based on demonstrable psychic phenomena, and evidence that life is eternal, unconditionally, through acceptable communication via mediumship, between this earthly physical plane and those residing in spirit only.

The realization that we do not change our personality or what we know (or others know) of our self, as we do our physical body at our transition to the spirit world, is a comfort, and yet because we are told through communication from those we know in spirit that we then must learn a new way to live, to improve our spiritual awareness in order for our innermost soul to become nearer to God, so we understand that as spirit now we have the opportunity to embark on that brighter path here and now.

Spiritualism teaches, with help from Guides, as they are commonly called, in the spirit realms, that we make what use we can of the physical body that houses us to be of service to God and to learn by first-hand experience.

Our spirit at physical death then utilizes a shelter of finer stuff to enable us to continue in our spiritual life, and then, when our spirit evolves more, the vibrations become finer and the etheric body is shed, and we move on yet again to a higher plane of existence.

So we progress from level to level in the fullness of spiritual time.

Spiritualism is also privy to the experiences of those in spirit themselves, who tell us that if the laws of nature are transgressed, the suffering thereafter is proportionate. We are not talking here of a human-imposed morality, but the unambiguous upholding of what our conscience tells us is right, to live in a positive state of 'good', with responsibility for our own thoughts, actions and the effect our lives have on the world at large, our planet and all its flora and fauna.

Spiritualists accept personal responsibility for their sins, and know that they must therefore personally atone for what they themselves must identify as wrong-doing.

Spiritualism states that heaven and hell are conditions of consciousness which can manifest here on earth as easily as in a future state of existence in spirit.

Life being the never ending-struggle to achieve love and wisdom, it is better to strive for that here than move on as a spiritually-deficient individual into the other dimensions.

The inescapable fact is that for every action there is a reaction, and if we have neglected those responsibilities towards promoting the best in ourselves and the good of our friends and companions in this life, there must be retribution in the next. Universal Justice will be done.

Spiritualist philosophy is constantly refuelled by new revelations from the higher realms of spirit, to which we should all aspire. It's this aspiration that raises us above our material composition to more spiritual consciousness, and an awareness of our spirit while we are still in the physical.

PRINCIPLES OF SPIRITUALISM

Our progression is in spirit, from dimension to dimension, plane to plane.

Spiritualism as a religion accepts nothing that cannot be demonstrated, therefore the concept of individuals in spirit, having once been on the earth plane, returning to the physical, which is also contradictory to the eternal progress in the realms of spirit which is open to all, is unacceptable.

Any follower of the orthodox and longer-established religions than the Spiritualist newcomer will be able to draw some parallels between their religion and Spiritualism.

Divine revelation, angels, those messengers from the higher realms of spirit, are in abundance in every monotheistic religion from Judaism to Christianity, Islam to Bahai. Prophets, those who could converse with angels, and holy (devoted to high ethical principles and God) individuals, who have mediumistic gifts, are there just for the looking.

Other less familiar religious groupings that we might term mystic belief systems, appear to have flourished on materialistic psychic powers, for instance Confucianism embraces the I Ching and other forms of divination, and the offshoot of that religion, founded by Confucius (his real name was K'ung Fu Tzu), is Taoism.

Taoists have in their time believed that disease is a result of sin and that the sick and disabled should be sent to prison! Although this sounds shocking to us, in those earlier times before humankind had any understanding of illness and its causes it was generally imagined that demons or the devil had entered the sufferer's body. Consequently the mystics and religious practitioners used to be called in to help. Psychic influence was brought to bear on the patient, the ancient forerunner of our spiritually-evolved modern-day Spiritualist Healing...

SPIRITUALIST HEALING

S piritualist healing encompasses all the aspects of Spiritualism as they apply to the material world, and demonstrates the fact that healing is effected by discarnate spirit without, focused through the spirit of the administering agent, the healer, to the spirit within the being who is in need of healing.

Of course all who are born require healing, as a condition of physical life. As William Shakespeare so aptly put it, we are subject to 'all the ills that flesh is heir to . . .'

Like very young children, the unsophisticated instincts of human beings at the beginning of human time on earth, having the capacity for much thought but having little and limited understanding of the world around them, allowed them to have a conscious awareness of themselves as psychic entities. Their existence being so close to the Original Source would have given them an almost indifferent attitude to the body in which they lived, apart from the absolutely basic fight-or-flight mechanism and procreatively-linked urges.

This is actually made plain by the simplified account of our beginnings in the Bible.

Because those early humans were so near to Creation itself, the inbuilt knowledge of spirit thought generating physical form produced the concept of the body at the mercy of not only its own spirit, but also, as a natural progression of ideas, that of the spirit forms of other physical – and unphysical or discarnate – beings.

In essence they were correct.

There's no doubt that there was an intuitive conception of attack by something living but with no soul or conscience (what we would now recognize as a germ, bacteria or virus), but the attendant, often ritualistic practices to stave off or drive out the attackers that caused the illness were way off beam.

Although physiologically-based medical science has advanced so slowly since the dawn of human history, when we consider some of the unethical uses to which this knowledge has been put we may be forgiven if some of us think it would have been better made even slower.

Given that our lives are spirit-driven, our minds being the consciousness of that spirit, and that the obtaining of information is collected and disseminated as a result of this process, all the scientific progress that has been made so far could be said to have been effected through the mind of the medical and scientific researcher, prompted by those to whose minds they are attuned to in the spirit world. As we think, so we attract.

It has always been a source of conjecture how more than one scientific investigator has come up with the same, usually highly revolutionary and innovative discovery at the same time. Baird and Marconi are two of the most famous of these synchronizations. However, by referring to the Spiritualist model of life, all 'coincidence' becomes clear.

So, the residents of the higher planes of existence – which must include the likes of John Logie Baird and Guglielmo Marconi – are indeed able to influence the physical world in which we live now, through spirit–mind there to spirit–mind here.

Although physicalists maintain that the mind is a function of the brain, Spiritualists understand that the seat of reason is spirit-based and sited in the etheric body.

While the brain allows physiological function which includes that which governs the physical processes of memory and experience, it is the mind alone that assesses these projected images and makes decisions.

Our mind appears to operate in three different but complementary ways. At one level it is concerned with the function of the physical incarnation, revealed for instance as that part which complains when the body is under stress – or is glad when it isn't...

Co-existent is the astral mind, so-called because of its affinity to the astral or higher spiritual plane. This aspect is the one that enables conscious detachment from any present physical situation, and works on a more objective vibration. It's thought that this particular part motivates and registers 'out of body' or 'near death' experiences, and also prompts those actions that can bring good or bad feelings, reactions and responses and is known to affect the physical self as well as the spiritual being. This area is also the repository of conscience.

The third section can be described as an intuitive zone that permeates the etheric and acts instinctively to protect the best interests of that spiritual life form. It is this energy field that picks up sensory information automatically and, without conscious recourse to thought, transmits and receives environmental messages via the customarily invisible auric field and etheric body.

The spirit body is in fact the perfect pattern for the physical life form, an eternal matrix composed of divine light that contains all the information necessary to maintain itself as an individual precinct, and with the capacity to store still more data, influencing its progress as a unique being.

PRINCIPLES OF SPIRITUALISM

Unlike the physically-manifested counterpart it has been proved by spiritually-divined means that when disturbed, either congenitally or traumatically, the etheric formation of our spirit body remains flawless.

Spiritualist healing for the physical being is effected by the use of spirit-side emanating forces and energies, conveyed on a sympathetic frequency, to a receiver, the healing medium, and transferred to the recipient by the laying on of hands, prayer or the directing of the medium's healing thoughts from a distance – a combination of all three can be quite usual.

All human beings are born with a natural instinct to heal, and to accept healing.

This is translated into physical touch, as we automatically place our own hands on any part of our body that hurts or is in any way uncomfortable, as the child is touched by its mother or another caring adult when it cries. 'Kissing things better' is much more than just an empty phrase.

But as my paternal grandmother used to say, 'If love could cure, we'd all be well.' Spiritualist healing is not a 'cure', but it helps, and that can make all the difference to someone who is suffering.

Its first effect is usually a marked lessening of pain, followed by a calmer and more tranquil feeling in the sufferer as a consequence, coupled with at least the beginnings of a more confident and positive attitude towards their situation.

All Spiritualist healing takes place because of this integral relationship between spirit and the body physical. A Spiritualist healing medium is keenly aware of the spirit and soul within those who come to them for help, and knows that the energy from spirit and the spirit world will first connect with the patient's inner being, to search out the problems therein.

Then as the calming and harmonizing vibrations will suffuse the soul and spirit, prompting a physical response, the person's suffering will ease up considerably.

There are of course many other forms of healing and therapies, but the Spiritualist healer acknowledges the origin of the
healing energies and knows that they are purely instruments,
or conduits, offered in the spirit of service to all humankind
and animal life.

THE SPIRITUALIST HEALER

A Spiritualist healer develops their mediumship through the
usual channels, and will have undertaken extra study to enable
them to extend their mediumistic parameters to include healing.

This extension of mediumship also includes practical work
as well as that of the theoretical variety, and while it is a satis-
fying aspect of the learning process it is also one which
requires firm commitment in the practical sense.

This also gives the aspiring Spiritualist healer proper
time to establish an attunement with those in spirit who will
be working with them, and, while they study the mechanics
of the service of healing alongside an experienced Spiritualist
healing medium, if they make a mistake not only can they be
advised on the spot, but the healing can be readjusted to no
one's detriment.

The student Spiritualist healer is also able to absorb the
working atmosphere, and come to terms with different energies and emotions they will experience in an environment
where Spiritualist healing is taking place.

Until the appointed teacher is satisfied that the student fully
understands their own role, as that of the passive exchange for
spirit healing activity, and of course the difference between
Spiritualist healing and other types which are not spirit-
directed but materially-based, a Spiritualist healing medium
will not be 'officially' allowed to work unsupervised.

If anyone wishes to consult a Spiritualist healing medium

privately, they should ask to see their qualification, which will be a certificate from a properly legally registered Spiritualist organization.

There are some who would say that they don't need any official recognition or such a seal of approval because they are natural, or are 'taught entirely by Guides', or 'do not need to study or read books', or that they 'have no need to ask anyone else for advice and guidance.' This could be construed as a negative attitude on the part of the would-be healer, and certainly plays no part in conventional Spiritualist healing practice. Spiritualist healers are also encouraged to take first-aid courses, as an earthly adjunct. If a self-declared healer won't read a book or take advice, how would they get on if someone suddenly fainted, or had a fall?

There has to be a desire to learn as much as is humanly possible, to strive for the best, to make a positive attempt to overcome self, so that those who wish to work with spirit helpers as part of their team will be so enabled.

LIKE ATTRACTS LIKE...

The development of mediumship is hard work and takes a lot of self-discipline, but is well worth the eventual outcome for all concerned – a Spiritualist healer who represents with dignity the living philosophy of Spiritualism, and puts it into demonstrable practice.

Even if someone has an obvious natural ability to tune in to the spirit frequencies, and receives inspiration and guidance from those quarters that overlay and enhance the gifts of spirit already apparent, extra knowledge is always better for the medium and the recipient, especially when that knowledge is applied to Spiritualist healing.

Spiritualist philosopher Arthur Findlay said that ignorance is a curse, and it's definitely a hindrance when it comes to highly evolved spirit input. Learning is crucial in some healing situations.

Every medium has a real duty to aspire to the highest level of expertise because they know that they might be the only one that a suffering person, or animal, may see, and so that single visit to a Spiritualist healing medium must count for as much as possible.

Spiritualist healers know that the healing ministry in spirit needs as highly developed workers on the earth plane as they can get, in order to provide the best for all those on earth, and this requires highly motivated individuals.

THE MINISTRY OF ANGELS

Spiritualism acknowledges the ministry of angels, and where better to espouse and demonstrate this tenet than within the context of healing?

By alleviating distress of the physical body, the spirit, or even the soul of someone incarnate through the ministry of higher spirit, the Spiritualist healer enjoys not only being the channel whereby another human being is experiencing physical and spiritual upliftment, but a taste of their own albeit passive partnership with those working for the good of all, on the other side of life.

LEGALITY

But even the agents of angels are regulated by earthly laws, and Spiritualist healers are particularly careful not to transgress these. Whether the laws applying to Spiritualist healers are all just, is another matter. In some European countries such as Germany, healing per se is illegal. Regulations that are ethically based are quite appropriate, however. A parent or guardian would be committing a criminal offence if they failed to provide adequate medical aid for a child under the age of 16,

and as healing is not 'medical aid' within the letter of the law, a Spiritualist healer would not be legally at liberty to treat a child if its parents refuse to enlist such medical aid. They could be accused of aiding and abetting such an offence.

As no one other than a qualified or training dentist should practise dentistry, Spiritualist healers are enjoined not to practise it, nor to give healing to women in actual childbirth or within 10 days thereafter.

Other than the fact that unqualified personnel should not be involved in such matters, I can't see why Spiritualist healing may not be given to someone in need, either as a result of a dental problem, labour or confinement, providing the necessary medically- and surgically-qualified people are also doing their own job.

Always bear in mind that Spiritualist healers should not offer their services, but wait to be asked.

Venereal disease sufferers may receive healing, but it must be without reward, either directly or indirectly – and of course we trust that they undergo the appropriate medical treatment in tandem.

It is totally legal to assist AIDS sufferers with Spiritualist healing.

SPIRITUALIST HEALING AS COMPLEMENTARY MEDICINE

Spiritualist healing is always given as a complementary therapy to orthodox medical techniques.

For the most part, Spiritualist healing is becoming more and more acceptable in Great Britain, and there have been two conferences on the role of complementary therapies to orthodox medicine, instigated by His Royal Highness The Prince of Wales, Prince Charles, and held at Buckingham Palace, to which for

the first time ever, representatives from the Spiritualists' National Union were invited.

Doctors are permitted to suggest or agree to one of their patients going to get extra help from a Spiritualist healer, provided they continue to receive whatever medical treatment is deemed necessary. Spiritualist healers are also becoming a more common sight in hospitals, although their discretion should ensure that if they have chosen to wear an overall, it is not white, which may give the false impression that they are members of one of the orthodox medical professions. A pastel shade of the rainbow is the more likely choice for the overall of a Spiritualist healer, or they may feel that such a garment isn't necessary at all.

A Spiritualist healer visiting a hospital, sanitarium or hospice environment is expected to conduct healing without bringing undue attention to themselves, perhaps holding hands with their patient and saying a prayer, so there is no embarrassment for anyone who has requested their services.

The Royal College of Veterinary Surgeons is accepting of animal healing by contact, laying on of hands, absent healing and prayer, however the responsible Spiritualist healer if called in to help an animal who obviously needs the services of a vet will advise the owner accordingly.

VISITING A SPIRITUALIST HEALER

As a first-time visitor to a Spiritualist healer, a patient will always be asked whether they have seen a medical doctor, and if they haven't will be advised so to do. If they have consulted a doctor, then they will *not* be told to discount that doctor's advice. If a Spiritualist healer is asked for their opinion on medical matters, forthcoming operations or drug prescriptions, they will reserve their own opinion and keep it to themselves.

94   Diagnosis is another 'no no', but if the Spiritualist healer suspects that their patient may have an infectious illness, they will advise them accordingly and not allow them to come into contact with anyone else waiting for treatment.

Clothing does not have to be removed for Spiritualist healing, unless it's shoes and a top coat, if the patient doesn't mind. Those who define themselves as qualified Spiritualist healers will not use hypnosis, massage or any kind of manipulation. If the patient has requested Spiritualist healing, regardless of what other qualifications in other complementary therapies the healer may have, Spiritualist healing is what will be given. Nothing else.

In fact there are painful conditions such as rheumatoid arthritis where massage is out of the frame altogether medically speaking, and hypnosis for someone who is addicted to some substance abuse or is otherwise mentally disturbed could have unforeseen results. Spiritualist healing is gentle healing.

It may be advised in some cases that absent, or distant, healing could be offered, instead of physical contact.

CONTACT HEALING

Contact healing is effected by, as its name suggests, the laying of the Spiritualist healer's hands on the patient's physical self.

This kind of contact is very pleasant for the recipient, who often feels a warm glow emanating from the hands of the Spiritualist healer to the parts that other therapies couldn't reach, and an enveloping feeling of being cared for – without condition.

It's an extremely energizing and relaxing experience, and one that some people like to repeat at regular intervals regardless of whether their original complaint has cleared up or has just been generally relieved.

Most physical conditions respond in a positive way to this

method of treatment, because of the benefit of human contact with a highly spiritually-motivated caring other and the almost indescribable physical sensation of angelic spirit working.

AURIC HEALING

Now this latter sensation also applies to those receiving Spiritualist healing via a medium delivering it, either solely or in part, through the physical auric energy field.

In fact, where a student Spiritualist healer is giving healing they will often render their assistance to spirit workers and their patient by doing so without touching the person but merely by allowing the healing to be directed through the aura.

This is an extremely workable arrangement for everyone involved, as the outcome will be just as positive and the trainee Spiritualist healer will have learned the different vibrations that surround those who are in need of specific healing, as well as those whose condition is non-specific, and will receive the first-hand knowledge that touching and physical manipulation is totally unnecessary in the pursuit of Spiritualist healing.

ABSENT HEALING

An extension of this is absent healing. This can be practised by a Spiritualist healer singly, at any time convenient, depending on the capacity of the medium to attune themselves to their helpers in the world of spirit.

Then there are those who meet in a group to send out their combined thoughts for those who are in need of help, perhaps suffering in mind or body, and for whom contact healing is not an option.

Spiritualist absent healing may be actually the preferred healing method for some mediums, and it is often noticeably successful, both when those at the receiving end are known to the instrumental mediums, and when such healing has been

asked for by relatives or friends on behalf of a loved one far away.

Many Spiritualist healers' groups churches and centres have absent healing books in which the names of anyone who needs healing can be written.

There is sometimes a healing prayer or invocation, for instance in some Spiritualist churches such as the one at Lewisham. This prayer is read out to the congregation attending the service before asking for healing for all those named in the book.

Some development circles also have absent healing books where members can put the names of those needing that service, and thoughts are sent out by the convening teaching Spiritualist medium at the appropriate time, and as part of the healing circle work when it meets.

Spiritualist healing can take place anywhere and at any time, as long as the healing medium is of the required high standard of attunement and concentration, although usually healing transpires in Spiritualist centres and churches on particular days of the week, and at regular times.

The procedural format will vary from place to place, sometimes dependent on what Spiritualist umbrella organization they belong to.

The common denominator is that they all offer the service of Spiritualist healing in similarly presented surroundings.

WHERE HEALING TAKES PLACE

Healing may take place in the main part of a church, in a side room or in a community centre's premises, such as a village hall or even a scout hut.

Wherever Spiritualist healing is on offer, the Spiritualist mediums who administer it will also ensure that the place in which they are to work is conducive to spirit healing energies and acceptable to those who come for that healing.

You can expect any room in which Spiritualist healing is to take place to be clean, airy, fresh-smelling and well lit.

There will be chairs for the recipients, and stools on which the healer(s) may sit for comfort while giving healing. Occasionally a couch is provided too, and fresh water to drink.

There will also be bowls of water, soap and hand towels for each individual healer, for although this is healing through non-physical agency, it is more hygienic for those who are in fairly close proximity to a succession of patients to wash their hands after each healing. Sometimes, though, it must be said, the Spiritualist healer may use the physical act of washing their hands to 'break the link' between clients, but of course they will have trained sufficiently well to be able to accomplish this link-breaking through mental discipline alone. It can also be a device for ensuring a little break for themselves, and to signal to waiting patients that it's soon going to be their turn!

The applicant for Spiritualist healing may be greeted by some soft music that puts them in the right frame of mind to be able to forget some of their everyday worries and relax a little while they wait to be attended to. Favourites at Lewisham on a Tuesday afternoon are *Silver Wings* and *Great Peace*; both are very soothing to listen to. After a couple of years of listening to these tape on a regular weekly basis, any of the healers there can tell the time without looking at a clock, and therefore how many more patients, or not, they can see before the end of the afternoon session. . .

In most Spiritualist healing venues a written record will be kept for the recipient of the Spiritualist healing ministry, and of course kept under lock and key as highly confidential. These serve to remind the medium involved of their patients' details, and over a period of time provide evidence of their progress, as well as aiding an appraisal by another Spiritualist healer

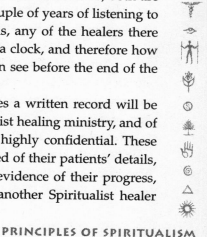

of the patient's story so far should the need for a change from their usual healer arise.

There are of course a multitude of spiritual healers in the British Isles who would not classify themselves as spiritualists, and that is fine for them, but the information herein is that which is relevant to Spiritualism and those who give service in its name.

In the former category are psychic healers.

Spiritualist healers allow energy from the higher realms of life to flow through them to their patient. The patient is, strictly speaking, placing him- or herself in the position of allowing God's will to work through those servants on both sides of the veil.

Spiritualist healers are no more exhausted when they complete their task than had they been undertaking any other similar physical exertion such as standing on their feet for hours in a shop, preparing and cooking a meal or driving for a couple of hours non-stop.

Psychic healers will feel extremely depleted after a session of healing, because they basically transfer their own energy to a person in need.

This is not a criticism of motive – who hasn't visited a loved one who is ill, and come away feeling shattered? It isn't only a psychological process, there has been a transfer of energy too. Life's energy fields are in the early stages of scientific detection as yet, but there is now some evidence to support what was previously considered a Spiritualist theory only.

There are some healers who maintain that they practise 'psychic surgery' – and actually use implements to cut and dig, apparently painlessly, at the people who consult them, to what usually in the long term – or even in the short, is no avail. Associated with this is the outward signs of spirit-controlled trance conditions. This is a sort of somnambulistic state in which some claim to be not just 'controlled' but 'inhabited' or 'possessed' by another entity, a separate personality from themselves who performs these pseudo operations.

Spiritualism is a religious philosophy that does not admit of irrational and illogical notions, and 'possession' of another's body space without permission comes high on the list of these irrational and illogical ideas.

As we are all body mind and spirit (not to mention our soul), and inextricably linked together until transition into the etheric world. Another entity cannot push the essential you out of the way against your will, nor make you do anything out of 'character'.

Certainly the aura is a vulnerable area, but all that's needed is to recognize our own individuality, and just like the shopkeeper or club owner who reserves the right to refuse entry to undesirable customers, the human being's individual space is sacrosanct and we can refuse ingress by trespassers.

Some who work in the trance state do allow their helpers to come very close to their physical self, almost like two in a bed, but this is a result of perfect love, trust and understanding.

The problem then with this kind of 'possession' is twofold: both ethical and legal.

The first is that there is an imbalance of power, and it may be that the spirit motivating and housed in the physical self of the medium is not as highly evolved or a spiritual as the other 'invited visitor'. Natural law does not permit any one in spirit to override another's free will or personality, and on consideration it then becomes clear why someone would utilize physical objects and tools while ostensibly carrying out 'psychic surgery'.

It is possible for a Spiritualist medium to be impressed by their Guides or helpers, to enable that special entity to express teachings and spiritual wisdom without having to fight their way past the medium's conscious thought-processes.

It is also possible for those in the spirit world to effect wonderful healing in this manner – but it is direct from spirit, sanctioned by the Highest, for reasons unknowable, and requires no physical ironmongery of any kind. It doesn't even need physical manipulation. There have been many amazing disappearances and shrinking of fibroids and tumours as a result of this sort of spirit intervention – and always for a reason, even if it is never fully understood.

People who should be in wheelchairs are still managing to walk about a little as a result of spirit ministrations; those who should be in constant pain with their afflictions aren't even feeling the need to take an aspirin tablet; children who were born 'without a chance' have survived against medical odds.

On the other hand, it isn't for anyone incarnate or indeed discarnate to say why some people live in the physical in a certain way, seemingly regardless of being given healing, and some seem to be more fortunate in their outcome of healing in their physical existence. There are surely many factors at work, including the social and economic conditions that many people find themselves in, and that it is incumbent upon humanity to try collectively to improve.

THE POWER OF GOOD

Spiritualist healing demonstrates the power of good, the existence of spirit here and now, and therefore the eternal nature of creation.

Spiritualist healing asks for no faith, either in the religious sense or in its application.

Spiritualist healing proves that belief in any creed doesn't affect the outcome of the healing ministry, because small children and animals are susceptible to improvement in their condition through such healing being applied to them, and they have no concept of a belief system or religious dogma.

Anyone can receive benefit from Spiritualist healing, whether they believe in God or not.

They do not need to have faith in a saviour, or perform any ritual prior to being given healing, and they can wear talismans or not, as they choose.

Faith healing is limited by asking for religious belief, Spiritualist healing is as unconditional as the love that generates it.

SPIRITUALISM IN THE 21ST CENTURY

All time is relative, and advent of a 2,000-year marker is only a fascinating but peripheral happening for those presently conscious of inhabiting the last half of the 6th millennium.

Even if we ignore the way in which the calendars of the world diverge between Western civilizations, the Eastern and the Middle Eastern, and provided that all of our years amount to approximately our planet's prescribed circuit round the solar system of about 365 days, do those of us who are living our earthly lives now really mind how many earth years have precisely passed? And when we look forward into our own future, tabulated finitely in earth time, can we grasp anything of the infinite and eternal that is to come?

It is only by recourse to our awareness of ourselves as spirit, who have emerged from and who are going back to the world of spirit, that we can hope to grasp the reality of time. That everything that was, and is now, will be in our collective future.

When we communicate with the multi-dimensional spirit realms, we converse into our own future, with those for whom life on the earth plane is in their past. So it is that we may receive insights into that future from those already living there.

One of the most common problems with any kind of prophecy that stems from this communication is the earthly time frame.

From the Spiritualist medium on a church platform who is asked by a communicator to tell their niece, in the evening's congregation, that there will be a house move in December, which the medium finds out later did take place, but not until the December three years further down the line; to the rather over-dramatic letter, so my mother thought, sent her by my father, that didn't make sense for 51 years. He told her he would 'leave this life today, February 1st' and that he would wait for her 'when she was grey-haired'.

He passed to spirit on February 1st 1991, and she passed two years later, when her hair was indeed sprinkled with silver.

So there is a window to our future through our spiritually-based contact with spirit, although we should not ask for it. We are told when it is deemed necessary. If the majority of, if not all, human beings were shown what was to happen to them throughout their lives on the earth plane, they would find it intolerable to contemplate. Yet if they were to be shown someone else's life and offered a swap, they would keep their own. . .

Spiritualism is a religion, a philosophy and a science, and as humankind approaches the next thousand years of its history the emphasis in the new age must be on science allied to spirituality, and the Seven Principles of Spiritualism.

The science of Spiritualism gives us a hint about why it came into existence when it did. The year 1848 was not only the beginning of a struggle for a new social order, but also of modern scientific discovery. The phenomena of Spiritualism can be explained by modern science. All living things occupy their special space in this world as varying energy systems within a greater energy order, and we know that energy is never lost but only changes form. Thought itself is a form of energy and, for example, it is this thought-field that attaches to an object which the psychometrist can pick up on. Thought-fields can act in a positive or negative way, in much the same way as a magnetic field, and so affect the mind. This can cause feelings of sickness – which fortunately responds well to absent healing!

There have been experiments to evaluate thought as energy fields, with successful outcomes, and this applies to forces outside our physical self.

Doctor S. R. Dean, speaking to the American Psychiatric Association in 1972, said: 'Thought is a form of energy; it has universal field properties which like gravitational and magnetic fields are amenable to scientific research. Thought fields survive death and are analogous to soul and spirit.'

Modern psychological theories also embrace otherwise 'mystical' experiences and pay systematic attention to non-ordinary states of consciousness.

Spiritualists know that mind is separate from matter, and that it is part of the spirit – and spiritual conformation. Spirit exists as much as the personality and, while in the physical body, can embellish and help it by drawing to its aid divine spiritual energy.

Vibration and frequency are now in common parlance, part of the technological advances made after 1848. The spirit realms are on a different vibration to our earthly space, and in scientific terms if a vibration is set up that equals that of a solid, it will destroy its structure, like the wine glass shattered by a high-frequency resonating musical note – or the walls of Jericho tumbled by the blast of a trumpet. For thousands of years before science was understood, spirit guidance told Joshua what to do to bring the wall down – and because he trusted what he heard from spirit it was accomplished, even though he could not have known then how it was effected.

Now even the most uninformed accept the reception of radio and television signals which, given a receiver, the radio or television set, enables them to hear music sent through thin air and watch people walking around in a box in their sitting room. Even so there is still a lingering assumption among human beings that if something cannot be seen or heard, touched or smelled, it doesn't exist.

This attitude applies to the sceptical when referring to spirit existence, but the fact is that science suggests that over 90 per cent of all matter in the universe is dark – invisible to us.

Nevertheless, Spiritualism, as a scientific religious philosophy, encourages genuine sceptical but open-minded enquiry. It was Herbert Spencer who said, 'There is a principle which is a bar against all information which is proof against all arguments, which cannot fail to keep a man in everlasting ignorance: that principle is contempt prior to investigation.'

The destructive effect that negative thought-waves can have, directed at, let us say, a Spiritualist medium who is attempting to bring evidence of survival to persuade that sceptic, or someone close, perhaps in a public arena, will usually be only too evident.

Others will only perceive a failure to produce proof of spirit and therefore be unconvinced of life after death, the mainspring of modern Spiritualism.

Spiritualism has been called a religion, a movement and a way of life.

To me Spiritualism is religion, a movement and life itself.

Spiritualism stands as a bulwark against the established religious dogmatists, the multitudinous and various rituals and trappings that are presently emplaced to underpin that orthodoxy in its many guises, and against the concept of any one of the entrenched sectarian belief systems claiming their revelation and methodology to be the only correct theology.

Spiritualism at its most apologetic claims to be the basis for all religions, in as much as the founders of these claims are, to a man, reported as having heard them from The Almighty direct, who it is then later inferred, having made pronouncement once, will not repeat what was previously said to anyone else.

Confident Spiritualism asserts that it is a universal religion, without ritual, without mysterious ornamentation and certainly without a male founding figurehead apparently requiring unquestioning obeisance to what was most obviously clairaudiently received dictat and revelation from the spirit world.

Because Spiritualism itself by its very nature is neither discriminatory nor polarized, it is able as a movement to embrace all the different, and differing, shades of opinion encountered within its remit.

As a progressive, forward-looking philosophy, Spiritualism is therefore able to admit humanists and atheists, monotheists and polytheists, so these non-discriminatory precepts may be perceived as a unifying and energetic force that provides the momentum necessary for any movement to take place.

Movement implies growth and progress. Spiritualism's emphasis on the positive side of life certainly supports this definition.

The mainspring of undying Spiritualism is love.

Not just experiential or selective love, but an all-encompassing, all-pervading eternal love. Although all life is commonly deemed to be a product of love, and to be demonstrably nurtured by love, Spiritualism further maintains that life continues sustained by love, albeit on another plane.

Within Spiritualism all may live as one, each individual sustained by a very real awareness and comprehension of the atmosphere generated by love.

PRINCIPLES OF SPIRITUALISM

Not only that, by utilizing this love exchange, Spiritualism provides demonstrations through its mediums that communication still transpires between Heaven and Earth, and all stages in between.

Mediumship is used to reunite friends and relatives from the etheric side of life with those still on the physical plane, thus proving survival after 'death', the basic tenet of Spiritualism. Mediums also receive philosophical and spiritual guidance to pass on as well as information from the highest planes that echoes and sometimes even reaffirms much that was given to the prophets of yore, and many good people since then.

Spiritualism is the oldest and the newest revealed interpretation of the condition called life.

Like the oldest religions, it was inspired into earthly inception by psychic phenomena, but, as befits a modern proposition, it does not demand blind faith or the passive acceptance of its survivalist philosophy, but actively encourages its adherents to look for the truth of the matter; to develop their own spirituality and/or psychic ability, to meet together with other like minds in order to facilitate any links with the world of spirit that may be available at the time, to pursue a pro-active course in an attempt to find and fulfil a purpose in this life for each enquirer, in order to make this world (and, as a consequence, the next world) a better place for all.

Spiritualism holds the key to universal survival.

Its predominantly orally-presented theistic philosophy, that God is all and in all things, embraces all other theologies.

That all are spirit and part of spirit discriminates against no other beings and no thing.

As a movement Spiritualism is beginning to make its presence felt. Its leading lights have yet to make public announcements on where Spiritualism stands on the issues of the day, but more and more individual affirmed Spiritualists are being invited on to the airwaves and into the public arena, so it can only be a matter of time now...

For sure and for the here and now, Spiritualism offers an alternative way of life which, if it were taken up by the majority of this world's population, would prevent its current headlong rush towards the disaster termed Armageddon in a message given by spirit to ancient mediums.

Spiritualism for me is life.

RESOURCE GUIDE

SOME SPIRITUALIST PUBLICATIONS, ORGANIZATIONS AND CENTRES

The Psychic News, Clock Cottage, Stansted Hall, Stansted, Essex CM24 8UD.

Two Worlds, 7 The Leather Market, Weston Street, London SE1 3ER.

The Spiritualists' National Union, incorporating The British Spiritualists' Lyceum Union, Redwoods, Stansted Hall, Stansted, Esssex CM24 8UD.

The Greater World Christian Spiritualist Association, 3–5 Conway Street, London W1P 5HA.

The Spiritualist Association of Great Britain, 33 Belgrave Square, London SW1X 8QB.

The White Eagle Lodge (London), 9 St Mary Abbots Place, Kensington, London W8 6LS.

The Institute of Spiritualist Mediums, Central Office, 3 Roding Leigh, South Woodham Ferrers, Chelmsford, Essex CM3 5JZ.

The International Spiritualist Federation c/o The SNU, General Secretary, Redwoods, Stansted Hall, Stansted, Essex CM24 8UD.

The Noah's Ark Society, 7 Sheen Close, Grange Park, Swindon SN5 6JF.

STUDY CENTRES

The Arthur Findlay College, Stansted Hall, Stansted, Essex CM24 8UD.

The Lynwood Fellowship, 36 Lady Frances Drive, Market Rasen, Lincoln LN8 3PH or Royes Ridge, 1 Plough Hill, Calstor, Lincoln LN7 6UR.

Lewisham Spiritualist Church, Boone Street, off Lee High Road, Lewisham, London SE13.

SOME MEETING PLACES FOR DIVINE SERVICES

The London Spiritual Mission Spiritualist Church, 13 Pembridge Place, London W2.

Rochester Square Spiritualist Centre (Sir Arthur Conan Doyle's Temple), Rochester Square, off Camden Road, London NW1.

Wimbledon Spiritualist Church, 136 Hartfield Road, London SW19 3TJ.

Westcliff National Spiritualist Church, Westborough Road, corner of Hildaville Drive, Westcliff on Sea, Essex SS0 9PZ.

Stockport Christian Spiritualist Church, 46 Old Road, Stockport, Cheshire SK4 1TD.

The Welling Spiritualist Centre, Community Hall, Wrotham Road, Welling, Kent.

Hampton Hill SNU Church, 12 Windmill Road, Hampton Hill, Middlesex.

Wath and West Melton Spiritualist Church, 6 Barnsley Road, Wath upon Dearne, nr. Barnsley, Yorkshire S63 7PY.

Stoubridge National Spiritualist Church, Union Street, off Hagley Road, Stourbridge, West Midlands.

Glasgow Association of Spiritualists, 6–7 Somerset Place, Sauchiehall Street, Glasgow G3 7JY.

Edinburgh Association of Spiritualists, 246 Morrison Street, Edinburgh EH5 8DT.

Belfast Spiritualist Church, 134 Malone Avenue, Co. Antrim, Northern Ireland BT9 6ET.

Littleport Spiritualist International Temple, c/o Rose Cottage, 51 Victoria Street, Littleport, Ely, Cambridgeshire CB6 1LY.

THE UNITED STATES OF AMERICA

SOME SPIRITUALIST PUBLICATIONS, ORGANIZATIONS AND CENTRES

The National Spiritualist Summit, 3251 W. Topeka Drive, Glendale, Arizona 85308-2325.

National Spiritualist Association of Churches, PO Box 217, Lily Dale, NY 14752-0217.

San Francisco Spiritualist Society, 1832 Buchanan, California.

Connecticut State Spiritualist Association, 101 Leffingwell Avenue, Waterbury 06710.

Denver Chapel of Spiritual Awareness, 1939 S. Monroe Street, Colorado 80210.

Orlando Spiritualist Church Awareness, 3210 N. Chickasaw Trail, PO Box 571043, Florida 32857-1043.

Salem, The Church of Spiritual Life, Masonic Hall, 109 Main Street, RT 97, New Hampshire.

The Journey Within (SNU kindred body/affiliated), PO Box 1413, Clifton, New Jersey 07015.